WITHOUT ADAM

THE FEMINA ANTHOLOGY
OF POETRY

It is difficult to believe anyone who says: "I have never composed a poem." The most prosaic man I ever knew was moved to compose a limerick on his honeymoon. It is the natural thing to do when stirred by an emotion on an aesthetic confrontation. But having done it, most people conceal the result. A few show it to selected intimates. Still fewer persuade someone to publish it. And a tiny minority make a business of it and are known to the world as poets.

Some poems are banal, like the poem of a wife inscribed on the tomb of her husband in Burford Church. But four added lines bring her into the company of poets:

"Love made me poet
And this I writ.
My heart did do it
But not my wit."

For young women who are often plagued by this itch to write poetry, it must be discouraging to find that the great poems they turn to, and the anthologies they browse in, are almost—not quite all, but almost—all the work of men. Yes indeed—the greatest *are* the work of men, and perhaps readers of Virginia Woolf's *A Room of One's Own* will think they know why. But very many women have been poets, and very many more should take heart and prove that they are poets. This new anthology of poems by women will encourage them.

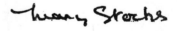

WITHOUT ADAM

THE FEMINA ANTHOLOGY
OF POETRY

Compiled by
JOAN MURRAY SIMPSON

A Femina Book

First published 1968 by Femina Books Ltd.

SBN: 85043 003 8

Distributed by Macdonald and Co. (Publishers) Ltd.
Gulf House, 2 Portman Street, London, W.1

Made and printed in Great Britain by
The Garden City Press Limited
Letchworth, Hertfordshire

ACKNOWLEDGEMENTS

Thanks are due to the Editors of *The Christian Science Monitor, Country Life, The Jewish Chronicle, The Listener, Manifold, Outposts* and *The Poetry Review* in which certain of the poems originally appeared, and to the poets, publishers and agents concerned for permission to print or reprint copyright poems as follows:

Oxford University Press for *Tigers* from *Tigers* by Fleur Adcock
Alice Alment for *On a Picture by Smith Haldy*
Marjorie Baldwin for *The Nature Lesson* from *The Slain Unicorn*
Frances Bellerby for *It Is Not Likely Now* from *The Stone Angel and the Stone Man* (Ted Williams, Plymouth)
Shirley Bridges for *So Few Sleep Soundly*
Vera Brittain for *We Shall Come No More*
The Cresset Press for *Ode on the Whole Duty of Parents* by Frances Cornford
Elisabeth Cluer for *The Last Enemy*
Marguerite Johansen Deane for *High-Heeled Boots*
Monica Ditmas for *Annunciation*
Elizabeth Dixon for *Ranmore*
Rosemary Dobson and Angus & Robertson Ltd. for *The Mirror* and *Azay-le-Rideau* from *Child With a Cockatoo* and *Country Press* from *The Ship of Ice*
Grove Press Inc. for Poem 5 from *The Flowering of the Rod* by Hilda Doolittle ('H.D.'). Copyright 1957 by Norman Holmes Pearson
Gervase Farjeon and Michael Joseph Ltd. for *The Girl With the Ball* by Eleanor Farjeon
Joan Forman for *For Sally*
Helen Forsyth for *Dichotomy*
Jean Overton Fuller for *Mask and Essence* from *Venus Protected* and *To a Young Man on his 30th Birthday*

Laurence Whistler for *Gloria in Excelsis* and *The Hare is Vanished* by Jill Furse

Karen Gershon and Eyre & Spottiswoode Ltd. for *Scene at Evening* and *On Planting a Tree* from *New Poets 1959*

Frances Gill for *Gulls* and *The Pennywhistle Man*

Rumer Godden for *Michaelmas Daisies*

Muriel Grainger for *The Scattering*

Rosamund Greenwood for *The Bairn* and *The Gift*

Madge Hales for *September*

Armitage Hargreaves for *Present Tense*

Phyllis Hartnoll for *A Death Abroad*

Kathleen Herbert for *The Virgin Capture*

Phoebe Hesketh and Rupert Hart-Davis Ltd. for *Epitaph, Rescue* and *The Serpent*

Barbara Vere Hodge for *The Night Light*

Dorothy Howard for *Eurydice*

May Ivimy for *On a Death in an Old People's Home* from *Midway This Path*

Sara Jackson for *The Window*

Elizabeth Jennings and André Deutsch for *Old Woman, The Diamond Cutter* and *Greek Statues*

Rosemary Joseph for *Going North for Christmas*

Jean Kenward for *Moorhens* from *A Flight of Words*

Angela Langfield for *The Chariot (Giacometti)*

Carla Lanyon Lanyon for *The Dunce* and *To My Godson*

Denise Levertov and Jonathan Cape Ltd. for *Come Into Animal Presence* and *Lonely Man*

Houghton Mifflin Co. for *Meeting House Hill* by Amy Lowell

Macmillan & Co. Ltd. for *The Question* from *Collected Poems* by Sylvia Lynd

The Executors of the Lilian Bowes Lyon Estate and Jonathan Cape Ltd. for *Northumbrian Farm* from *Collected Poems*

Ross Macaulay for her translation of Sappho's *Ode to Aphrodite*

Phyllis McGinley and Secker & Warburg Ltd. for *Ballroom Dancing Class* from *Love Letters of Phyllis McGinley*

Marion Marlowe for *The Trout*

Erica Marx for *Speeding Ship* from *Escape from Anger*

William Collins Sons & Co. Ltd. for *The Crystal Tree* from *All About Cyphers* by Phyllis Mégroz

Pamela Melnikoff for *The Lighthouse at Acre*

George Duckworth & Co. Ltd. for 40 lines from *Madeleine in Church* by Charlotte Mew

The Executors of Alice Meynell and Burns & Oates Ltd. for *Regrets* by Alice Meynell

J. Dallyn for *Sympathy* by Viola Meynell

Mrs. Norma Millay Ellis for *An Ancient Gesture* and *Thou Famished Grave* from *Collected Poems*, Harper & Row. Copyright 1928, 1934, 1939, 1954, 1955, 1962, 1967 by Edna St. Vincent Millay and Norma Millay Ellis

Charlotte Mitchell for *May Day* from *Twelve Burnt Saucepans*

Faber & Faber Ltd. for *What Are Years?* from *Collected Poems* by Marianne Moore

Miss S. Skrine for *A Bud in the Frost* by Moira O'Neill

Mary Oliver and J. M. Dent & Sons Ltd. for *No Voyage* and *The Grandmothers* from *No Voyage and Other Poems*

The Viking Press Inc. for *Ultimatum* from *The Portable Dorothy Parker*. Copyright 1931, 1959 by Dorothy Parker

Betty Parvin for *Gulls Aground*

Elise Passavant for *Thoughts on the Unicorn* from *Desert Places*

Rita Peck for *Fishmarket*

Ruth Pitter and The Cresset Press Ltd. for *The Unicorn*, *The Swan Bathing* and *Vision of the Cuckoo*

Miss Olwyn Hughes for *Tulips* and *The Moon and the Yew Tree* from *Ariel* by Sylvia Plath

Kathleen Raine and Hamish Hamilton for *Statues* and *Images* from *The Hollow Hill*, Copyright 1965 by Kathleen Raine; Hamish Hamilton, London

Celia Randall for *Harvest*

Sylvia Read for *The Dark Rider* and *Pictures*

Vera Rich for *The Bronze of Poseidon*

Faber & Faber Ltd. for *The Gaze* and *A Matter of Life and Death* from *A Matter of Life and Death* by Anne Ridler

Nigel Nicolson for an extract from *The Land* and *Full Moon* by Victoria Sackville-West

Denise Salfeld for *Ballad of the Handsome Man* from *Ballad of the Handsome Man*

Barbara Noel Scott for *Stillbirth* and *The Wild Poppies*

Griselda Scott for *Joseph and the Magi*

7

E. J. Scovell for *Child Waking* from *The River Steamer*

Anne Sexton and The Oxford University Press for *Unknown Girl in the Maternity Ward* from *Selected Poems*

Miss E. Maitland for *The New Ghost* by Fredegond Shove

Macmillan & Co. Ltd. for *The Swans* and *Heart and Mind* from *Green Song* by Edith Sitwell

Stevie Smith and Longmans Green & Co. Ltd. for *The Dedicated Dancing Bull and the Water Maid* and *Anger's Freeing Power* from *The Frog Prince and Other Poems* and for *My Hat*

Rita Spurr for *The White Horse*

Maida Stanier for *Freshmen* and *Hiawatha's Pancake* from *Free and Easy*

Margaret Stanley-Wrench for *A Visitation, In the Radiotherapy Unit* and *Hinterland*

Jan Struther and Chatto & Windus Ltd. for *Glamour*

Alice V. Stuart for *Water Lily on Loch Bran* (George Ronald 1953)

Jean Symons for *Elegy*

Odette Tchernine for *The Leopard*

The Macmillan Co. for *Effigy of a Nun* from *Collected Poems by Sara Teasdale*, Copyright 1926 by the Macmillan Company, renewed 1954 by Mamie T. Wheless

Rosemary Tonks and Putnam & Co. for *Story of a Hotel Room* from *Notes on Cafés and Bedrooms*

The Society of Authors and Miss Pamela Hinkson for *Larks* by Katherine Tynan

J. M. Dent & Sons Ltd. for *Mountain Flora* from *Theophanies* by Evelyn Underhill

Constable Publishers Ltd. for two translations from *Medieval Latin Lyrics* by Helen Waddell

Executors of the Mary Webb Estate and Jonathan Cape Ltd. for *Swallows* and *Fairy Led* from *Poems and the Spring of Joy* by Mary Webb

Dorothy Wellesley's Literary Estate and The Hogarth Press for *Swannery* from *Lost Planet*

Anne Welsh and the Oxford University Press for *Sight* from *A Book of South African Verse*

J. G. C. Hepburn for *The Fired Pot* by Anna Wickham

Diana Witherby and André Deutsch for *The Leafy Day* from *The Heat and the Cold*

CONTENTS

NOCTURNES AND MEDITATIONS

15

FOREWORD

This anthology is for everyone who cares about poetry and even for those who are still a bit doubtful, but it is dedicated in particular to the young people of our time in the hope that it may serve as an encouragement and an inspiration. It is an undeniable fact that in all the other anthologies that come our way the percentage of women contributors is exceedingly low, and in the whole field of educational books the emphasis is predominantly masculine. It is hoped that this anthology may serve to redress the balance a little and to show what women have accomplished and are accomplishing in one field of the arts.

A friend of mine, after being subjected to prolonged scrutiny by a small child in a bus, was baffled to hear, in a stage-whisper : "Mummy, what is that man *for*?" Faced with the same question about poetry, one might say that at its best it serves to deepen our understanding, to intensify our joy and to increase our sense of kinship with all living things. High goals indeed, but in preparing this anthology I have kept them in mind, while leaving room for laughter and gaiety as well. In order to please everyone, a good armful of flowers (which is after all what the word 'anthology' means) should include not only the tall lilies and perfect roses but some simple daisies and pungent field flowers as well.

Since the body of poetry is growing all the time it is of course impossible to produce a definitive anthology by women poets, and in the final analysis any compilation is bound to reflect personal taste, but I have tried to make this anthology as representative as possible.

In two cases permission was withheld as the poets seemed to feel some shame in joining a group consisting of women only, and in the case of some of the greatest Americans the high cost of copyright regrettably prevented us from including a larger selection of their work.

17

It often seems that anthologies have been prepared from other anthologies but in this one I have tried to select fresh poems from the poets' own collected works and hope that readers will be led on to study more of the work of writers they may meet here for the first time. Notes on points of special interest (indicated by an asterisk after the poet's name) are arranged alphabetically at the end. Dates are given for poets no longer with us.

There are no *poetesses* represented in this volume. Those of us who happen to be women as well as poets resent the label. It seems to smack of condescension—as if what we write had some kind of pink ribbon round it to distinguish it from the work of men.

With some obvious and deliberate exceptions, these poems are not specifically feminine in outlook. They are here, not primarily because they were written by women, but because they were written by poets, or by those who have, under pressure of emotion or event, been enabled to write true poems. I believe that all poets have what Keats called 'negative capability'—the power to become that which they contemplate, to partake of the essence of things through the imagination. The point I hope to make is that there is no artificial division between men and women where the art of poetry is concerned, no lower range at which the female alone can operate.

There is surely a happy medium between the opposite belligerences of *'Vive la Différence!'* and 'Anything you can do I can do better!' and in the belief that we have found it, we present with confidence the Femina Anthology.

JOAN MURRAY SIMPSON

18

PEOPLE

ODE ON THE WHOLE DUTY OF PARENTS

The spirits of children are remote and wise,
They must go free
Like fishes in the sea
Or starlings in the skies,
Whilst you remain
The shore where casually they come again.
But when there falls the stalking shade of fear,
You must be suddenly near,
You, the unstable, must become a tree
In whose unending heights of flowering green
Hangs every fruit that grows, with silver bells;
Where heart-distracting magic birds are seen
And all the things a fairy-story tells;
Though still you should possess
Roots that go deep in ordinary earth,
And strong consoling bark
To love and to caress.

Last, when at dark
Safe on the pillow lies an up-gazing head
And drinking holy eyes
Are fixed on you,
When, from behind them, questions come to birth
Insistently,
On all the things that you have ever said
Of suns and snakes and parallelograms and flies,
And whether these are true,
Then for a while you'll need to be no more
That sheltering shore
Or legendary tree in safety spread,
No, then you must put on
The robes of Solomon,
Or simply be
Sir Isaac Newton sitting on the bed.

FRANCES CORNFORD
(1886–1960)

21

THE DUNCE

That boy in the seventh row at the secondary modern
Is, as usual, not attending.
On the blackboard, the simple sums
(Glorified by the name of Mathematics)
Have no interest, on a summer day, for him,
And are therefore beyond the comprehension
Of one so obviously sub-standard.

His father cuts chestnut branches for fences,
Pollards willows, bends back and binds the strong boughs of
    hedges,
Clears forest undergrowth or brambles from ditches;
Steady jobs but not very remunerative.
His son is just an idler in the country;

A boy who has found the twin eggs of the night-jar
Tenderly handled, egg-shell breakable
Though they look like hard cemetery marble.
He can lead you to wild rare orchids, wine red violets—
Or gentian clumps in August. His toys are leaf skeletons,
Oak-apples, lords-and-ladies in the lane banks.

He knows which wood is burning by the smell of it,
What bird is singing by the notes it sings,
Who owned the moulted wing-feather, what creature
Shed that twist of fur caught in the wire barb;
And his eyes are seldom on the blackboard
When he is thinking of all these things :

Thinking of spiders' overnight invasion,
Their thousand parachutes hung on the blackberries,
Of the eyed-hawk-moth, patterned like tree-bark
And little things that live between bark and trunk
Who scatter on fourteen legs if you prise their roof off.
The trouble is, that lad lacks concentration.

He has an innocence beyond his years
Who has seen a vixen instructing her cubs at twilight
Or courting weasels dancing a pas-de-deux
In dawn dew; and sometimes in his ways has come upon
Two human lovers lying in the yew wood.

But all this store of extraneous knowledge
(Including, alas, the lovers)
Is totally unlearnt by the teacher of mathematics
And utterly useless for the eleven plus.
That ignorant child is a waste of good education;
He had better be just a woodsman like his father.

CARLA LANYON LANYON

HIGH-HEELED BOOTS

Here am I—tall as the pine-tree.
I lick the clouds, I swing by the rainbow,
I walk on my high heels—so high, so high.
I stretch my arms—
My shoulders brush the East and the West.
The little grey people run between my fingers.
The city crawls beneath my stride.
I laugh, and the chimneys shake,
I curse, and the pavements cringe.
I walk up and down in the night on my high heels,
So tall, so tall.
The wind swoons in my floating hair—
My long hair—Will you measure it?
Can you see the trail of it across the sky?
I will net the stars in my long hair
As I walk through the night on my high heels . . .

23

Past the girls on the pavements,
Girls with hair spilling over their faces,
Girls with teasing eyes and tempting shapes.
I pass them—tall, tall in my high-heeled boots.
My shoulders brush the East and the West,
The chimneys quake and the pavements cringe—
But I hear them laugh.
Why does she laugh, the pale-eyed blonde?
Girls should not laugh—no woman should mock.
She should cast down her eyes and tremble.
She should not pout her breasts and shake her hips,
She should not tease the giant in his passing.

What has happened to the pale-eyed blonde?
Red are the broken mouths that gape in her breast,
Red is the sweat of my hands and the blade is red.
Girls with long, blonde hair spilling over their faces—
Why should they mock, why should they jeer—
For am I not tall—
Tall, tall, in my high-heeled boots—
And my shoulders, do they not brush the East and the West?

But the room is so narrow
And the sky has come down upon me.
Officer, find my mother.
Will she be in now—now that the sky is down?
She was never in when the stones hit me,
When they bruised my face and I cried for her—
Officer, find my mother—
For to her I shall still be tall,
Tall, tall, as the pine-tree on the hill,
Tall as the shadow running before the rainbow—
To her ah, still so tall!—
Though I measure no more than a mouth to drown at her
    breast.

MARGUERITE JOHANSEN

24

TO MY GODSON

My infant godson, I would teach you other things,
Besides the Lord's Prayer in the vulgar tongue,
To learn along the years that lead to manhood,
Small lowly lessons, the unvirile virtues :
So now I wish you only humility.

May you hear sometimes, in those unrecorded hours
Between midnight and morning, when old men die
And young men dance and babes whimper for the breast,
Hear the pity-filled laughter of angels
For all that masculine magnificence, the pomp
Of epaulets and orders, mitre, gown and wig
To clothe the uncertain, shivering, naked form
Of man, proud man.

Choose humility, choose it if you dare
To stand without the fancy-dress support
Of platform dignity, cocked-hat importance.
Now you have two short names, titles enough
To serve your God with and to love your neighbour.
May you live long in meekness, unrewarded,
And may there be no obituaries at your death.

CARLA LANYON LANYON

FOR SALLY

Love, in my wood, the small child sings—
The sunlit child, my sister's child—
She clasps the leaves and claps her hands,
And puts her small hands round her knees,
And sings the songs my sister sang,
And I sang, too—and you, and you—
When life was innocent and new.

25

She lives the songs and small-bell rhymes
That speak to me of ancient times :
They speak to her of now and here,
They bear no undertones of fear.
She does not hear the indrawn breath;
Has never heard the cold word, "Death".

Love, in my wood, the small child sings,
(The sunlit child, my sister's child)
The songs we all sang, hopeful, guessing,
Believing life was flowered with blessing.
Stand in the shadow, poet, so
She may sing on, and never know.

JOAN FORMAN

TO A YOUNG MAN ON HIS THIRTIETH BIRTHDAY

(For Timothy d'A. S.)

The twenties are too much sung; the nine years
That have gone by since one's majority
Can leave the best part of one's destiny
Still to discover. A shadowed road veers
And a whole new landscape, still unguessed, appears,
That lies in the sun. Believe my prophecy,
Who rounded a huge headland, to find surprisedly
White roads ran all ways; better nears.

Deer whose polished horns are now emerging
From the velvet : the vulnerable vesture
That was soft and sensitive and bled
And bruised easily throughout the spring
Is rubbing off, to let the bone transfigure.
Hart now four-antlered, lift a new tooled head.

JEAN OVERTON FULLER

26

THE GRANDMOTHERS

They moved like rivers in their mended stockings,
Their skirts, their buns, their bodies grown
Round as trees. Over the kitchen fires
They hoarded magics, and the heavy bowls
Of Sunday bread rose up faithful as light.
We smiled for them although they never spoke.
Silent as stones, they merely stared when birds
Fell in the leaves, or brooms wore out, or children
Scraped their knees and cried. Within my village,
We did not think it odd or ask for words;
In their vast arms we knew that we were loved.

I remember their happiness at the birth of children.
I remember their hands, swollen and hard as wood;
And how sometimes in summer when the night
Was thick with stars they gathered in the garden.
Near sleep, I watched them as they poured the wine,
Hung paper lanterns in the alien birches.
Then one would take the tiny concertina
And cradle it against her mammoth apron,
Till music hung like ribbons in the trees
And round my bed. Oh, still within my dreams,
Softly they gather under summer stars
And sing of the far Danube, of Vienna,
Clear as a flight of wild and slender girls!

MARY OLIVER
(u.s.a.)

THE PENNYWHISTLE MAN

Beneath awkward branches clipped of birds,
A small house two shelves from the ground
Shakes its cracked windows at the trains.
Washing limps against its mast,
Old men talk and smoulder their gardens;
The chocolate painted gates, opening
On to each new freedom, are gone.
The lawn is a shanty for cockerels
And the people are variegated.
Then through a pattern of some ancient rain
The wall of years is down,
And with Sunday hands I twist
The plants to impossibilities.
Perhaps to remember is to imagine
But the day seemed bright,
The sea on the china plates rippled a little
As I watched my grandmother watch the window.
I saw him first, since my eyes were new to horizons—
And as he raised his arms, dabbled plumage to the sun,
To blow the flat, breathy tune over the fence—
This was the sunlight of my Sunday,
While the ribbon at my grandmother's throat grew tight
And her hands, thick white feathers
Fluttered over the coins on the table.
When he had gone, an old hunched bird
In the gutter of life, I never asked why
He only played for us, and why there was so much money
For such brief, bad music. And when I knew
The sunlight of my Sunday was in the lanes,
I was in the tree of his arm, and the knowing was nothing.
But now the tears in my head go back
To the eyes of the child, and are wept at last.

FRANCES GILL

BALLAD OF THE HANDSOME MAN

The tall, tall and handsome man
Who walked upon the shore
And swung his cloak and twirled his cane
Is walking there no more.

Grey and white the water shone,
Grey and black the sky,
With a scarlet lining to his cloak
The handsome man strolled by.

Oh, tall man with pale hair,
Walking by the sea,
You sing so much and sing so loud
And will not speak to me.

Oh, handsome man with piercing eye
As bright and hard as stone,
You watch the waves come rolling in
While I stand alone.

Far, far the sands are spread,
Flat and sleek and wet.
No use to look for passing feet
The sands will soon forget.

Fast and strong the wind blew,
The waves ran up the shore.
The tall, pale and handsome man
Is walking there no more.

He twirled his cane and swung his cloak,
The scarlet lining shone.
The sand remains, the rocks remain,
The handsome man is gone.

DENISE SALFELD

JOSEPH AND THE MAGI

Joseph the Stepfather,
Joseph forbearing, slow
To put away his lately chosen bride,
Accepted the angel,
Let the story go,
Choosing belief to ease a lover's pride.

Joseph new married
Had the nine months to muse,
To query the angel whether truth or dream.
Accepting the coming child
Yet must he question whose—
How likely did divine conception seem?

Joseph the stepfather,
Joseph run soft with love,
Plied the small fingers of another's son;
Accepted the charge of him,
Fearing lest features prove
The actual fatherhood, the guilty one.

Joseph the hurt of heart,
Sunk in his doubting, felt
Faith flooding home when men of wisdom claimed
His child their awaited Christ.
With three from the East he knelt—
Joseph the faithless shamed.

GRISELDA SCOTT

EFFIGY OF A NUN

Infinite gentleness, infinite irony
Are in this face with fast-sealed eyes
And round this mouth that learned in loneliness
How useless their wisdom is to the wise.

In her nun's habit carved patiently, lovingly,
By one who knew the ways of womankind,
This woman's face still keeps, in its cold, wistful calm,
All of the subtle pride of her mind.

These long patrician hands clasping the crucifix
Show she had weighed the world, her will was set;
These pale curved lips of hers, holding their hidden smile,
Once having made their choice knew no regret.

She was of those who hoard their own thoughts carefully,
Feeling them far too dear to give away,
Content to look at life with the high insolent
Air of an audience watching a play.

If she was curious, if she was passionate,
She must have told herself that love was great,
But that the lacking it might be as great a thing
If she held fast to it, challenging fate.

She who so loved herself and her own warring thoughts,
Watching their humorous, tragic rebound,
In her thick habit's fold, sleeping, sleeping,
Is she amused at dreams she has found?

Infinite tenderness, infinite irony
Are hidden forever in her closed eyes,
Who must have learnt too well in her long loneliness
How empty wisdom is, even to the wise.

SARA TEASDALE
(U.S.A.)
(1884–1933)

ROUEN

Why did no-one say it
    was like this?
These cobbles smoking
still with the shame of her burning,
and the mediaeval houses leaning
    with shuttered eyes
    and shuddered looks.

Today the people are unreal
they are the shadows
who drift the square.
Only the ghosts live. Their spirits
clamour for our attention, the guilty
    soldiers shout
    the silent crowds cry out.

There is a market behind
her white statue,
the suppliant stone
compels the clamorous thoughts
of butter and Normandy cheese bought
    with frugal care,
    to an awareness of prayer.

At her feet are flowers,
flat little wreaths
where the flames licked
first, of the country flowers she knew
and must have loved when child she grew
    so soon to a saint's
    stature and restraint.

She must have been
a difficult person
to live with, knowing
herself to be right, having her voices
at her elbow. The people had no choice
    but to call her
    witch, and staked, burn her.

Even now, it is awkward
being English, and taking
photographs. We speak
French, quietly, hoping we are unnoticed. They
did not put in the Guide that the grey
        square still cried
        so long after she died.

TULIPS

The tulips are too excitable, it is winter here.
Look how white everything is, how quiet, how snowed-in.
I am learning peacefulness, lying by myself quietly
As the light lies on these white walls, this bed, these hands.
I am nobody; I have nothing to do with explosions.
I have given my name and my day-clothes up to the nurses
And my history to the anaesthetist and my body to surgeons.

They have propped my head between the pillow and the sheet-
    cuff
Like an eye between two white lids that will not shut.
Stupid pupil, it has to take everything in.
The nurses pass and pass, they are no trouble,
They pass the way gulls pass inland in their white caps,
Doing things with their hands, one just the same as another,
So it is impossible to tell how many there are.

My body is a pebble to them, they tend it as water
Tends to the pebbles it must run over, smoothing them gently.
They bring me numbness in their bright needles, they bring
    me sleep.
Now I have lost myself I am sick of baggage—
My patent leather overnight case like a black pillbox,
My husband and child smiling out of the family photo;
Their smiles catch on to my skin, little smiling hooks.

I have let things slip, a thirty-year-old cargo boat
Stubbornly hanging on to my name and address.
They have swabbed me clear of my loving associations.
Scared and bare on the green plastic-pillowed trolley
I watched my teaset, my bureaus of linen, my books
Sink out of sight, and the water went over my head.
I am a nun now, I have never been so pure.

I didn't want any flowers, I only wanted
To lie with my hands turned up and be utterly empty.
How free it is, you have no idea how free—
The peacefulness is so big it dazes you,
And it asks nothing, a name tag, a few trinkets.
It is what the dead close on, finally; I imagine them
Shutting their mouths on it, like a Communion tablet.

The tulips are too red in the first place, they hurt me.
Even through the gift paper I could hear them breathe
Lightly through their white swaddlings, like an awful baby.
Their redness talks to my wound, it corresponds.
They are subtle : they seem to float, though they weigh me
    down,
Upsetting me with their sudden tongues and their colour,
A dozen red lead sinkers round my neck.

Nobody watched me before, now I am watched.
The tulips turn to me, and the window behind me
Where once a day the light slowly widens and slowly thins,
And I see myself, flat, ridiculous, a cut-paper shadow
Between the eye of the sun and the eyes of the tulips,
And I have no face, I have wanted to efface myself.
The vivid tulips eat my oxygen.

Before they came the air was calm enough,
Coming and going, breath by breath, without any fuss.
Then the tulips filled it up like a loud noise.
Now the air snags and eddies round them the way a river
Snags and eddies round a sunken rust-red engine.
They concentrate my attention, that was happy
Playing and resting without committing itself.

The walls, also, seem to be warming themselves.
The tulips should be behind bars like dangerous animals;
They are opening like the mouth of some great African cat,
And I am aware of my heart : it opens and closes
Its bowl of red blooms out of sheer love of me.
The water I taste is warm and salt, like the sea,
And comes from a country far away as health.

SYLVIA PLATH
(U.S.A.)
(1932–1963)

IN THE RADIOTHERAPY UNIT

No, she's not lying down there now for love
With her knees drawn up, face sideways on the pillow,
And loose hair slopping over the edge of the bed.
Look, and you'll see the sunlight has gone out of it,
Brittle and dry as winter grass. Not birth,
Not lust, not sleep makes her lie down like this.
There's growth in her still, another sort of intrusion
Into the body where a man's lust thrust,
A child grew, over whose skin a lover's hand
Moved gently, softly, like water, sun or rain,
That body, probed by all the claims that pluck
And claw and pull and sap a woman's living.
Now the last claim has pushed her on this bed,
And will choke her breath and close her mouth, as once
A Lover's kiss sealed, clogged the quivering tongue.
Yet my throat chokes with compassion, not for this,
But at the small, formal, housewife's smile, politely
Greeting the nurse like a guest on the doorstep, using
Light, inadequate words, and meeting death
Perhaps, with the same grave, sweet, pure courtesy,
Decorous courage; this, not agony
Cuts to the human bone, is not to be borne.
O this, this, lovers alive on the hot bed

Struggling to the dark light, the burning centre,
Remember it, and let, like rain, sun, water,
Tenderness move over your fragile bodies,
For you are lost, as she is, and alone.

MARGARET STANLEY-WRENCH

NO VOYAGE

I wake earlier, now that the birds have come
And sing in the unfailing trees.
On a cot by an open window
I lie like land used up, while spring unfolds.

Now of all voyagers I remember, who among them
Did not board ship with grief among their maps?—
Till it seemed men never go somewhere, they only leave
Wherever they are, when the dying begins.

For myself, I find my wanting life
Implores no novelty and no disguise of distance;
Where, in what country, might I put down these thoughts,
Who still am citizen of this fallen city?

On a cot by an open window, I lie and remember
While the birds in the trees sing of the circle of time.
Let the dying go on, and let me, if I can,
Inherit from disaster before I move.

O, I go to see the great ships ride from harbour,
And my wounds leap with impatience; yet I turn back
To sort the weeping ruins of my house :
Here or nowhere I will make peace with the fact.

MARY OLIVER
(U.S.A.)

36

THE FIRED POT

In our town people live in rows.
The only irregular thing in a street is the steeple;
And where that points to, God only knows
And not the poor, disciplined people!
And I have watched the women growing old,
Passionate about pins, and pence and soap,
Till the heart within my wedded breast grew cold,
And I lost hope.
But a young soldier came to our town,
He spoke his mind most candidly.
He asked me quickly to lie down,
And that was very good for me.
For though I gave him no embrace—
Remembering my duty—
He altered the expression of my face
And gave me back my beauty.

ANNA WICKHAM
(1884–1947)

AN ANCIENT GESTURE

I thought, as I wiped my eyes on the corner of my apron :
Penelope did this too.
And more than once : you can't keep weaving all day
And undoing it all through the night;
Your arms get tired, and the back of your neck gets tight;
And along towards morning, when you think it will never be
    light,
And your husband has been gone, and you don't know where,
    for years
Suddenly you burst into tears;
There is simply nothing else to do.

And I thought, as I wiped my eyes on the corner of my apron :
This is an ancient gesture, authentic, antique,
In the very best tradition, classic, Greek;
Ulysses did this too.
But only as a gesture,—a gesture which implied
To the assembled throng that he was much too moved to speak.
He learned it from Penelope . . .
Penelope, who really cried.

EDNA ST. VINCENT MILLAY
(U.S.A.)
(1892–1950)

LE BONHEUR

(for the film by Agnès Varda)

The sensual children sucking drowsy thumbs
Heavy with sleep, with love,
Feel the earth's pull like pears.
Eden itself lies all about them still
Where they move innocent as milk, passionate as peaches,
Their sexuality purposeless.

The mother-breast, dark-nippled, huge as earth
Is far from love-play now.
The mother-hands comfort and guide,
Straighten and fold, lift and lay down,
Make beds make food make garments,
Their purposes the purposes of love.

Life has one purpose only—to make life.
The tenderness of man is incidental,
A decoration, like the lyre-bird's nest.
Only in high romance is love exclusive—
Any kind form will serve :
From the first kiss all the rest follows—

38

Hollow and height, limbs mingling,
Contours of bone and flesh familiar as bread,
Startling as water in sunlight.
This is the dance of life, absurd yet grave,
Private, untellable, never to be divulged,
Repeating yet never the same, like waves or flames,
Repeating like flames or waves,
Like waves or flames . . .

JOAN MURRAY SIMPSON

ELEGY

The sun is setting, dear people. The slight
Wash of a boat fades, the lake mist rises,
Far away car doors slam.
We picnicked on chicken and brown bread and lettuce and
    peaches.
Let us wait here for a little together, look—
(The sun is setting)
Look how the evening light grows thick and softer
Than lake water and softer
Than inside chestnut shells and richer
Than plum nearest the stone but dark and soft.

I saw you proud young man with an old face
Swing down from the hill with chestnut branches and oak
    branches.
I saw you young women bend
Over, intent on the water, you became landscape,
Air and sun and reflection gave you their being.
We waded far out,
Fish lipped our feet, we dipped the peaches
For cleanliness, they took fish-scale colour—
Gleaming air envelopes grew in their bloom
And rose swinging and curving

39

The path smelt of peach. Dust
Clung to wet ankles and dried again and fell free,
We climbed to the short grass, and talked,
The day is lost in the night like words in air.
Collect together litter we used and made,
Smooth out the paper,
Dear people it will be cold, we must go
Down now, I must go this way now, and you
Reach home safely, you
Drive softly along the edge of this still lake.

JEAN SYMONS

LONELY MAN

An open world
    within its mountain rim :
trees on the plain lifting
    their heads, fine strokes
    of grass stretching themselves to breathe
the last of the light.
                        Where a man
riding horseback raises dust
    under the eucalyptus trees, a long way off, the dust
is gray-gold, a cloud
    of pollen. A field
    of cosmea turns
    all its many faces
of wide-open flowers west, to the light.

It is your loneliness
your energy
            baffled in the stillness
    gives an edge to the shadows—
the great sweep of mountain shadow,
shadows of ants and leaves,
    the stones of the road each with its shadow

40

and you with your long shadow
closing your book and standing up
to stretch, your long shadow-arms
   stretching back of you, baffled.

DENISE LEVERTOV
(U.S.A.)

THE TWINS

Not because of their beauty—though they are slender
as saplings of white cedar, and long as lilies—
not because of their delicate dancing step,
or their brown hair sideways blown like the manes of fillies—
it is not for their beauty that the crowd in the street
wavers like dry leaves around them on the wind.
It is the chord, the intricate unison
of one and one, strikes home to the watcher's mind.

How sweet is the double gesture, the mirror-answer;
same hand woven in same, like arm in arm.
Salt blood like tears freshens the crowd's dry veins,
and moving in its web of time and harm
the unloved heart asks, "Where is my reply,
my kin, my answer? I am driven and alone."
Their serene eyes seek nothing. They walk by.
They move into the future and are gone.

JUDITH WRIGHT
(Australia)

COUNTRY MATTERS

from THE LAND

I sing the cycle of my country's year,
I sing the tillage, and the reaping sing,
Classic monotony, that modes and wars
Leave undisturbed, unbettered, for their best
Was born immediate, of expediency.
The sickle sought no art; the axe, the share
Draped no superfluous beauty round their steel;
The scythe desired no music for her stroke,
Her stroke sufficed in music, as her blade
Laid low the swathes; the scythesmen swept, nor cared
What crop had ripened, whether oats in Greece
Or oats in Kent; the shepherd on the ridge
Like his Bœotian forebear kept his flocks,
And still their outlines on our tenderer sky
Simple and classic rear their grave design
As once at Thebes, as once in Lombardy.

The country habit has me by the heart,
For he's bewitched forever who has seen,
Not with his eyes but with his vision, Spring
Flow down the woods and stipple leaves with sun,
As each man knows the life that fits him best,
The shape it makes in his soul, the tune, the tone,
And after ranging on a tentative flight
Stoops like the merlin to the constant lure.
The country habit has me by the heart.
I never hear the sheep-bells in the fold,
Nor see the ungainly heron rise and flap
Over the marsh, nor hear the asprous corn
Clash, as the reapers set the sheaves in shocks
(That like a tented army dream away
The night beneath the moon in silvered fields),
Nor watch the stubborn team of horse and man
Graven upon the skyline, nor regain
The signposts on the roads towards my home
Bearing familiar names—without a strong
Leaping of recognition; only here

Lies peace after uneasy truancy;
Here meet and marry many harmonies,
—All harmonies being ultimately one,—
Small mirroring majestic; for as earth
Rolls on her journey, so her little fields
Ripen or sleep, and the necessities
Of seasons match the planetary law.
So truly stride between the earth and heaven
Sowers of grain : so truly in the spring
Earth's orbit swings both blood and sap to rhythm,
And infinite and humble are at one;
So the brown hedger, through the evening lanes
Homeward returning, sees above the ricks,
Sickle in hand, the sickle in the sky.

VICTORIA SACKVILLE-WEST
(1892–1962)

NORTHUMBRIAN FARM

Early and very early, by a moon dawn-dimmed,
Go clinking to the milking farmer and hind.
Hardily hands unwind
The silk-soft milk, the frothing fairy skein;
Gnomes on the lime-washed wall, for generations limned
By ritual lantern's light we wax and wane.

Slovenly-great the old bull wakes
To his contracted kingdom, shakes
The straw from his lustreless flank in fiery flakes.
Men scatter to far fields, to the ten-acre stubble,
To the hedge-sickle and plough;
Heavily beats now
Our bull's huge heart left pondering; his decadence makes
Morning come slowlier; grizzled Time in trouble.

46

Pastureward covetous-eyed creep
The cows again, with udders easy and slack;
Each leaves her track
Her snail's track on a world still hoar with sleep.
The half-shot-away hare
(Mark, Gentlemen of England now abed!)
Stitches a precious thread
Of blood into the upland turf—oh learning to be dead.

You see, we lose the knack.
After the black furrow (there's no turning back)
Silvery lapwing, pied plover weep
And weave a wild consolation crying Enough said,
Oh weave, child, weave a bravery through despair.
Here's speedwell too, as though the blue sky bled.
Most beauty is signed with sorrow; the iron share
Though it strike fire from flint, bites deep.

LILIAN BOWES LYON
(1889–1956)

ENVY

His life is umber.
From earth colours olives grow,
Are lopped, are cultivated.
The whole family, their backs half broken,
Sweat into wool, or women's headscarves,
Bullying the fields, longing
For factory work, and shops and the good pavements.

Blurred, crushed
By noise and traffic, here we cough
From smoke and the corroding fumes
Or stand, tired out, in hateful wetness; dreaming

Of vines and the sweet chestnut trees.
O envy of simple poverty,
Of maize hung up, of heaviest hoe, of sun.

SHEILA WINGFIELD

HARVEST

Only the stubble is left where the barley,
Swept by the wind, was a golden sea,
Only a bevy of starlings, dark gleaners,
Trouble the air with the movement of wings.
Where the last gleam of sun strikes the doorway,
The old farmer sits, his hands on his knees,—
Hands gnarled like old tree roots, hands that once laboured,
Strong at the plough, and the scythe, and the binding,
Hands that are still. The daylight is fading,
And slowly rising, he feels for his stick,
And makes for his chair by the fireside, content,
With his granaries filled, and the harvest well gathered.
'Likely his last', thinks his granddaughter, passing,
Proud in her young days, to suckle her child.

CELIA RANDALL

COUNTRY PRESS

Under the dusty print of hobnailed boot,
Strewn on the floor the papers still assert
In ornamental gothic, swash italics
And bands of printer's flowers (traditional)
Mixed in a riot of typographic fancy,
This is the *Western Star*, the Farmer's Guide
The Voice of Progress for the Nyngle District.

Page-proofs of double-spread with running headlines
Paper the walls, and sets of cigarette-cards
Where pouter-bosomed showgirls still display
The charms that dazzled in the nineteen hundreds.
Through gaping slats
Latticed with sun the ivy tendrils fall
Twining the disused platen thrust away
Under a pall of dust in nineteen-twenty.
Draw up a chair, sit down. Just shift the galleys.
You say you have a notice? There's no one dies
But what we know about it. Births, deaths and marriages,
Council reports, wool prices, river-heights,
The itinerant poem and the classified ads—
They all come homewards to the *Western Star*.
Joe's our type-setter. Meet Joe Burrel. Joe's
A promising lad—and Joe, near forty-seven,
Peers from a tennis-shade and, smiling vaguely,
Completes the headline for the Baptist Social.
The dance, the smoke-oh, and the children's picnic
Down by the river-flats beneath the willows—
They all come homewards and Joe sets them all,
Between the morning and the mid-day schooner.
Oh, *Western Star* that bringest all to fold,
The yarding sales, the champion shorthorn bull,
And William's pain-relieving liniment,
When I shall die
Set me up close against my fellow-men,
Cheer that cold column headed "Deaths" with flowers,
Or mix me up with Births and Marriages;
Surround the tragic statement of my death
With euchre-drives and good-times-had-by-all
That, with those warm concomitants of life
Jostled and cheered, in lower-case italics
I shall go homewards in the *Western Star*.

ROSEMARY DOBSON*
(Australia)

49

The teacher has the flowers on her desk,
Then goes round, giving one to each of us.
We are going to study the primrose—
To find out all about it. It has five petals,
(Notice the little dent in each, making it heart-shaped)
And a pale green calyx (and O! the hairy stem!)
Now, in the middle of the flower
There may be a little knob—that is the pistil—
Or perhaps your flower may show the bunch of stamens.
                    We look at our flowers
To find out which kind we have got.

Now we are going to look inside,
So pull your petals off, one by one.
                    But wait . . .
If I pull my flower to pieces it will stop
Being a primrose. It will be just bits
Strewn on my desk. I can't pull it to pieces.
What does it matter what goes on inside?
I won't find out by pulling it to pieces,
Because it will not be a primrose any more,
And the bits will not mean anything at all.
A primrose is a primrose, not just bits.

It lies there, five-petalled primrose—
A whole primrose, a living primrose.
To find out what is inside I make it dead,
And then it will not be a primrose.
                    You can't find out
What goes one inside a living flower that way.
The teacher talks, fingers rustle . . .
I will look over my neighbour's flower
And leave my primrose whole. But if the teacher comes
And tells me singly to pull my flower to pieces
Then I will do as I am told. The teacher comes,
Passes my neighbour on her gangway side,
Does not see my primrose is still whole,

50

Goes by, not noticing; nobody notices.
My flower remains a primrose, that they all
Want to find out about by pulling to pieces.
I am alone : all the world is alone
In the flower left breathing on my desk.

MARJORIE BALDWIN

WATER LILY ON LOCH BRAN

The lochan in the mild September sun
Lay pooled in its own peace; no sough of wind
Stirred the dark ridge of pines on the further shore,
No ripple ran through the birches, thinly scattered
On the nearer verge, their slight, their feminine leaves
Already faintly goldening to autumn.

On the blue pool, open to the eye of heaven
That beamed upon it from a flawless sky,
Lay a water-lily; the white waxen cup
Rode silently, like a little ship at anchor,
Resting upon its leaves, and gently rocked
Now and again, in the secret wash of the waters.

Gazing upon its life, so lightly moored
To earth in the fluid element of water,
Its single purpose steadfast in that chalice
Upheld to the warm beneficence of heaven,
I knew why the ancient East devised the lotus
As the perfect type and symbol of contemplation.

ALICE V. STUART
(Scotland)

THE WILD POPPIES

Still they burn on, the wind-sown poppies,
A last flicker of summer, in my garden.
I left them, liking their lazy flame
And coarse black gipsy eye, and even the scent
That is like the sweat of sleep.
Now they have braved
November. I shall let them burn away
And scatter the living ash from their dry urns.

All my life, I have weeded, cultivated, planted,
Trimmed to the commonplace, said the right things.
Perhaps when I am old and surly as this sun
That leans across the wall of my grey garden
Not caring much, I shall find it growing still—
Whatever it was in me that no one wanted
But myself—the weed I liked and never cared to kill.

BARBARA NOEL SCOTT

SEPTEMBER

Apples in gales drop like footsteps
Like thunder rain thud without cease
So watch out for your head! they fall
Hard that grow high. We take hop baskets

Gather the green turning yellow
The red, dusky, sweet as briar smell.
New blackbirds stutter near, aggressive
Drive off the old. The grass

Bruises like apples. The basket clutches
Fruity balls. I see them like yesterday's
Child. My hair winds like a scarf. The
Wind makes me laugh. Unwind the scarf.

September whirls in blown death throes.
I am dying. I am old in September.
And winter has hollows for eyes. The
New blackbirds face winter unknowing.

Bending and picking apples I am shorter
than dwarfs. The thin light stays where fruit
Lies. Like satin and silks the peel blooms
And glows. Some are brown bumped like artichokes.

I feel continuance bending and picking apples.
There is no end. This garden is for always.
I know fruit smells as I know roses or nightstock.
All is now. This moment. As it always will be.

MADGE HALES

MICHAELMAS DAISIES

This is St. Michael and all angels weather,
all the bright host of air and water
sparing the earth these thin dry days
and the ghost of fire sent up in woodsmoke.
It is a holiday
and a holy day;
the sun-haze is the halo of the saint's visitation,
a halo on the hedges, on blackberries and sparrows;
he has the stillness of an autumn crocus
but for his insignia, the michaelmas daisies.

Nothing is itself but doubled in sun,
and their colours burn
with arch-angel meanings :
purple for royalty,
crimson for courage,
lint-white for purity,
violet for homage.

He is the fighting angel, defending heaven,
but now heaven is here on earth;
his sword is in the sunset
tempered to shepherd's delight,
at night his shield is blazed with stars;
his legs, straddling the world, have loosed their greaves,
we stack them with the stooks of autumn sheaves
as he stands, swinging the censer
of the full ripe earth before the altar
of the days that are steadily coming,
harvest of saints and souls,
and Advent growing
to the cock-crow of a new world;
but the incense is broken off now,
these days and minutes,
motes of September;
and sprinkled for his own savour
this brilliance of daisies;
royalty,
courage,
purity,
homage,
incense on incense in every garden.

RUMER GODDEN

RANMORE

So you are all contradiction,
October trees.
That birch by the brambly track
Was a swarm of golden bees.
This destitute whitebeam's up
To the ankles in litter, of paper-chase,
A shock like the first snow.
But now in this dip the woods are holy,
Heavy with incense, and sun

54

Netted through layers on layers of green
Or scissoring through
So light and green make a fourth dimension
(As candle and plainsong in the dark do).
And here one beech one
Phoenix in ecstasy gives up itself,
Surrenders and achieves the sun,
A blazing incarnation.

ELIZABETH DIXON

SIGHT

A shine and shock
Are scarlet lilies
By sun-dazzled waters.
Storm-bloom on hills,
Rock-sparkle or bright glass—
Each colour is a cock
That crows of glory.

Sun sprays new fibres
On leaf-cool collections,
And golden butterflies
Dance on a dusty surface.
Rivers are pliant light
Or stanchions for sun.
Grasses, ivory, or rose,
Stones, apricot, or red
Smoulder to pale miles overhead.

Out of the crowded valley's colour
Single call-notes trumpet as I pass,
Till eyes are strutting peacocks,
And sharp mosaics
Block out distance
Where no fronds wave.

In glittering valleys
Shine is more lucid than argument,
Horizons make an arbitrary ring,
And this closed-circuit for the eyes
Sets all the roundelays.

Distance is silent—
It is beyond sight.
O mountains not seen, can I recognise,
Or even discover your colours
When articulate trumpets are missing?

ANNE WELSH
(South Africa)

POEM FROM LLANBYRI

If you come my way that is . . .
Between now and then, I will offer you
A fist full of rock cress fresh from the bank
The valley tips of garlic red with dew
Cooler than shallots, a breath you can swank

In the village when you come. At noon-day
I will offer you a choice bowl of cawl
Served with a 'lover's' spoon and a chopped spray
Of leeks or savori fach, not used now

In the old way you'll understand. The din
Of children singing through the eyelet sheds
Ringing 'smith hoops, chasing the butt of hens;
Or I can offer you Cwmcelyn spread

With quartz stones, from the wild scratchings of men;
You will have to go carefully with clogs
Or thick shoes for it's treacherous the fen,
The East and West Marshes also have bogs.

Then I'll do the lights, fill the lamp with oil,
Get coal from the shed, water from the well;
Pluck and draw pigeon with crop of green foil
This your good supper from the lime-tree fell.

A sit by the hearth with the blue flames rising,
No talk. Just a stare at 'Time' gathering
Healed thoughts, pool insight, like swan sailing
Peace and sound around the home, offering

You a night's rest and my day's energy.
You must come, start this pilgrimage,
Can you come?—send an ode or elegy
In the old way and raise our heritage.

LYNETTE ROBERTS
(Wales)

A NOCTURNAL REVERIE

In such a Night, when every louder Wind
Is to its distant Cavern safe confin'd;
And only gentle Zephyr fans his Wings,
And lonely Philomel, still waking, sings;
Or from some Tree, fam'd for the Owl's delight,
She hollowing clear, directs the Wand'rer right :
In such a Night, when passing Clouds give place,
Or thinly vail the Heav'ns mysterious Face;
When in some River, overhung with Green,
The waving Moon and trembling Leaves are seen;
When freshen'd Grass now bears itself upright,
And makes cool Banks to pleasing Rest invite,
Whence springs the Woodbind and the Bramble-Rose,
And where the sleepy Cowslip shelter'd grows;
Whilst now a paler Hue the Foxglove takes,
Yet checquers still with Red the dusky brakes :
When scatter'd Glow-worms, but in Twilight fine,

Shew trivial Beauties, watch their Hour to shine;
Whilst Salisb'ry stands the Test of every Light,
In perfect Charms, and perfect Virtue bright :
When Odours, which declin'd repelling Day,
Thro' temp'rate Air uninterrupted stray;
When darken'd Groves their softest Shadows wear,
And falling waters we distinctly hear;
When thro' the Gloom more venerable shows
Some ancient Fabrick, awful in Repose,
While Sunburnt Hills their swarthy Looks conceal,
And swelling Haycocks thicken up the Vale :
When the loos'd Horse now, as his Pasture leads,
Comes slowly grazing thro' th'adjoining Meads,
Whose stealing Pace, and lengthen'd Shade we fear,
Till torn up Forage in his Teeth we hear :
When nibbling Sheep at large pursue their Food,
And unmolested Kine rechew the Cud;
When Curlews cry beneath the Village-walls,
And to her straggling brood the Partridge calls;
Their short-liv'd Jubilee the Creatures keep,
Which but endures while Tyrant-Man does sleep;
When a sedate content the Spirit feels,
And no fierce Light disturbs whilst it reveals;
But silent Musings urge the Mind to seek
Something, too high for Syllables to speak;
Till the free Soul to a compos'dness charm'd,
Finding the Elements of Rage disarm'd,
O'er all below a solemn Quiet grown,
Joys in th'inferiour World, and thinks it like her Own :
In such a Night let Me abroad remain,
Till Morning breaks, and All's confus'd again;
Our Cares, our Toils, our Clamours are renew'd,
Or Pleasures, seldom reach'd, again pursu'd.

ANNE FINCH, COUNTESS OF WINCHELSEA*
(1661–1720)

WHAT DOES SHE DREAM OF?

What does she dream of, lingering all alone
   On the vast terrace, o'er that stream impending?
Through all the dim, still night no life-like tone
   With the soft rush of wind and wave is blending.
Her fairy step upon the marble falls
With startling echo through those silent halls.

Chill is the night, though glorious, and she folds
   Her robe upon her breast to meet the blast
Coming down from the barren Northern wolds.
   There, how she shuddered as the breeze blew past
And died on yonder track of foam, with shiver
Of giant reed and flag fringing the river.

Full, brilliant shines the moon—lifted on high
   O'er noble land and nobler river flowing,
Through parting hills that swell upon that sky
   Still with the hue of dying daylight glowing,
Swell with their plumy woods and dewy glades,
Opening to moonlight in the deepest shades.

Turn lady to thy halls, for singing shrill
   Again the gust descends—again the river
Frets into foam—I see thy dark eyes fill
   With large and bitter tears—thy sweet lips quiver.

CHARLOTTE BRONTË*
(1816–1855)

LINES COMPOSED IN A WOOD ON A WINDY DAY

My soul is awakened, my spirit is soaring
And carried aloft on the wings of the breeze;
For above and around me the wild wind is roaring,
Arousing to rapture the earth and the seas.

The long withered grass in the sunshine is glancing,
The bare trees are tossing their branches on high;
The dead leaves, beneath them, are merrily dancing,
The white clouds are scudding across the blue sky.

I wish I could see how the ocean is lashing
The foam of its billows to whirlwinds of spray;
I wish I could see how its proud waves are dashing,
And hear the wild roar of their thunder today.

ANNE BRONTË*
(1820–1849)

HIGH WAVING HEATHER

High waving heather, 'neath stormy blasts bending,
    Midnight and moonlight and bright shining stars;
Darkness and glory rejoicingly blending,
Earth rising to heaven and heaven descending;
Man's spirit away from the drear dungeon sending,—
    Bursting the fetters and breaking the bars.

All down the mountain-sides wild forests lending
    One mighty voice to the life-giving wind;
Rivers their banks in the jubilee rending,
Fast through the valleys a reckless course wending,
Wilder and deeper their waters extending,
    Leaving a desolate desert behind.

Shining and lowering and swelling and dying,—
    Changing forever, from midnight to noon;
Roaring like thunder, like soft music sighing,
Shadows on shadows advancing and flying,
Lightning-bright flashes the deep gloom defying
    Coming as swiftly and fading as soon.

EMILY BRONTË*
(1818–1848)

SHALL EARTH NO MORE INSPIRE THEE?

Shall earth no more inspire thee,
Thou lonely dreamer, now?
Since passion may not fire thee,
Shall nature cease to bow?

Thy mind is ever moving
In regions dark to thee;
Recall its useless roving;
Come back, and dwell with me.

I know my mountain breezes
Enchant and soothe thee still,
I know my sunshine pleases,
Despite thy wayward will.

When day, with evening blending,
Sinks from the summer sky,
I've seen thy spirit bending
In fond idolatry.

I've watched thee every hour;
I know my mighty sway :
I know my magic power
To drive thy griefs away.

Few hearts to mortals given
On earth so wildly pine;
Yet few would ask a heaven
More like this earth than thine.

Then let my winds caress thee;
Thy comrade let me be :
Since nought beside can bless thee,
Return—and dwell with me.

EMILY BRONTË*
(1818–1848)

61

CREATURES

COME INTO ANIMAL PRESENCE

Come into animal presence.
No man is so guileless as
the serpent. The lonely white
rabbit on the roof is a star
twitching its ears at the rain.
The llama intricately
folding its hind legs to be seated
not disdains but mildly
disregards human approval.
What joy when the insouciant
armadillo glances at us and doesn't
quicken his trotting
across the track into the palm brush.

What is this joy? That no animal
falters, but knows what it must do?
That the snake has no blemish,
that the rabbit inspects his strange surroundings
in white star-silence? The llama
rests in dignity, the armadillo
has some intention to pursue in the palm-forest.
Those who were sacred have remained so,
holiness does not dissolve, it is a presence
of bronze, only the sight that saw it
faltered and turned from it.
An old joy returns in holy presence.

DENISE LEVERTOV
(U.S.A.)

A VISITATION

"Come quickly, quickly!" The words
Flew up the well of the staircase,
Through the cage of the banister's white bars.

And I ran down as quickly
In case, in case . . .
There, on the doorstep, on the old, worn stone
Was a toad like a stone, a brown and ancient stone,
Crouched close, and blinking his bright amber eyes.
It was as if the garden was there, the essence
Of earth and growth, exuding through the house
Something much older than the worn rind of bricks
And warped wood. He looked so warm, like earth,
The heart fluttering gently, he basked in the sunlight
In my hand he would have been cold, weight and burden
A cold heart. Untouched, he moved away
Leaving for a moment his moist shadow
A blessing on the lintel. Now the lungwort's
Large freckled leaves stirred up on my rockery,
Breathed, were still. The air was purged and healed.
Should I have poured a libation? Who was he?
The golden eye had wisdom, and was older
Than ours, evasive and too vulnerable.
The house breathed also. Leaves blew in and lay
There, on the floor, like creatures. Up the stairs
Sounds, shadows, light
Flew up and perched. All was open now.
The lintel like a god's stone, worn and warm,
Needed no wine or oil, only the sun
And stumbling feet that fret, bless, and caress.

MARGARET STANLEY-WRENCH

THE SWAN BATHING

Now to be clean he must abandon himself
To that fair yielding element whose lord he is.
There in the mid-current, where she is strongest,
Facing the stream, he half sinks, who knows how?

His armed head, his prow wave-worthy, he dips under :
The meeting streams glide rearward, fill the hollow
Of the proud wings : then as if fainting he falls sidelong,
Prone, without shame, reveals the shiplike belly
Tumbling reversed, with limp black paddles waving,
And down, gliding abandoned, helplessly wallows,
The head and neck, wrecked mast and pennon, trailing.

It is enough, satisfied he rears himself,
Sorts with swift movement his disordered tackle,
Rises, again the master : and so seated
Rising, with spreading wings he flogs the water
Lest she should triumph : In a storm of weeping
And a great rainbow of her tears transfigured,
With spreading circles of his force he smites her
Till remote tremblings heave her rushy verges
And all her lesser lives are rocked with rumour.

Now they are reconciled : with half-raised pinion
And backward-leaning head pensively sailing,
With silver furrow the reflected evening
Parting, he softly goes : and one cold feather
Drifts, and is taken gently by the rushes :
By him forgotten, and by her remembered.

RUTH PITTER

SWANNERY

I well remember the swan's nest
at the end of the long lake
Above Roche Abbey (that first daughter of Fountains)
Where for weed we could not row.
I remember the anger of the great swan,
When the sun was down,
And we two children in twilight, trying to row.

I remember the lake with the maps of lilies
That were hands to drag us down,
We cared only for the pride of the great swan.
We watched his anger rejoicing,
The anger of his sirehood
On the lake above Roche Abbey,
And we trying to row.

The children have died long ago
But the swan has not gone.
It is good that we saw the swan
And the maps of lilies that grow
Between a child and a swannery.

I hail him, whose sires heard
The cry of the Ave Maria
Arising from woods and waters,
Above Gothic ruins undying;
On the lake above Roche Abbey.

I hail him, the angry bird
I hail his anger, his aristocracy
In this world spiritually dying.
I hail the pride of the swan.
He reigns yet, we are gone.

DOROTHY WELLESLEY
(Ireland)

MOORHENS

It is the pool that first accepts the season's
Lusty approaches, frothing fresh as wine
With the huge shape of frogs and shiftless, airy
Bladders of quaking spawn, clotted with fine

Spots like a woman's veil. It is the water
That quickens first, having at last discarded
Her sheath of ice. Now, sleek as caramel
She loosens subtly under the sun's spell . . .

Never the same, her smooth disseminating
Corrugation broaches the shore's brim,
Where a moorhen, small as coal, beats his important
Journey—as though the world were hinged on him—
Tug-like and brisk. For here, too, the eternal
Fever of getting and begetting burns;
And in the sedge his mate broods, dark as marble,
And in the pool the marbled sky returns.

JEAN KENWARD

THE LEOPARD

The leopard was snow in the winter grief
Where the ice-fall broke on his flank like a knife
That touched at the place where the heart should be
And was in the moment of fear in life.
The watchful jewel, once savage eye,
Now softened to thaw where the heart was struck,
Sheathed were the claws in calamity
Of the upper heights as the sky breathed rare
On a sharpness like freezing blades laid bare.
Velvet the moan in the creature's throat
Pleading for comfort, some kindred note.

But once in the warmth of the valleys again
Of green, where the prey and his own kind walked,
The ravaged heart of high loneliness
Became the prowling spur that stalked
The innocent, weak, and unaware.

69

And on that sun-gilt coat as bright
As unreal peaks receding white
With the great and massive clouds upchurned,
Through the fur the mark of his kind returned
While the inborn senses to jungle burned.

Loneliness still, but familiar the scent
Of tall spear grass, of tree fork bent
Where the predator crouched, unwinking stare
Of his amber eyes searching everywhere.

ODETTE TCHERNINE

THE LEAFY DAY

The fallow deer are filtering along the tangled track,
They push beyond the ferny turns, and soon have disappeared,
Dappled inside thickness of the thin new trees.
The children clink and chatter upon the gravel road,
Their heads are warm, like marigolds, and orange in the sun,
But sometimes they will follow where their long long shadows
    lead,
So they swerve across the ditch, where the light is hushed by
    beech
To lean, in green enveloped, and feel the solitude
(As they never feel again) of the spider drily rustling
On the dim-lit forest floor. The deer remain invisible,
Their overloaded antlers and vulnerable fur ears
Are faced towards the footsteps, muffled in moss,
While the sky moves back and forwards on this harmless leafy
    day.

DIANA WITHERBY

THOUGHTS ON THE UNICORN

(The poem referred to is B. S. Johnson's 'A Dublin Unicorn')

Taking one poem to make another
may be judged a compliment,
or an impertinence—depends
on how you look at it.
There is a magic in the theme
that over-rides the reasoning.
As if the mount had got the bit
between its teeth, and galloped off
to music of its own.

The poem haunts me and all night
I waited. But the unicorn
has passed to where the spring corn stands,
for no scent came to him from where
I slept. He might have paused, performed
some service. There is always need
for purity, if not for homage.

Now it is dawn and I am walking
in another pair of shoes.
The story stays right through the day's
distractions. I remember reading
that the unicorn does not
produce his kind, and so died out.
But all the same, I can imagine
his excitement at the scent
of the young virgin, disregarding
danger. Trust can always be
offered, even if betrayed.

There may be softer ways to die
than in the act of love, an arrow
through the heart, that can be either
love or death, can also be
a kind of purity, a cleansing.

71

So I wait. They say he makes
a sound like little bells, but it
is morning, and the hooves of night
have left their imprint on the grass.
I listen. In the echo of
remembered lines, far down the fields
I hear a hunter's horn.

I have pursued the unicorn
into the desert places, where
the mind shifts from reflection to
reality. Mirages that
may lead to death or madness. So
I wait beside the brackish water.
One day he may come
and purify the pool,
and I may drink.

ELISE PASSAVANT

THE VIRGIN CAPTURE

I fed upon flowers, the pungent essence of grasses
Sweetened my breath, my hooves beat through the bare
Springland of the generous earth, I mounted the hinds
That ran like smoke in the path of my morning glory,
The brush of my lion's mane emblazoned the air.

I froze in my tracks as the horn fractured my forehead,
Hurt, and at bay, the burst of the single bud
Fiery and unexpected, pre-electing the gain
Of my luminous white and wondering difference. Wary,
I pawed at the ground as the terrible probe drew blood.

When it was fully grown, delicate, slender,
I moved with new intent, the weight on my brow

72

Tenderly arching my neck; patient and calm
I trod with my spell-bound hooves the archaic story
Of the lonely legendary beast. Incorruptible now

I came to the place where she sat, virginal, gentle,
Her eyes, as she turned, tempered the mystical trap
To my brute surrender, her hand softened the pain
Of the single fabulous horn, the solitary journey;
My knees broke to her side, I laid my head in her lap.

KATHLEEN HERBERT*

GULLS

Silent, scuffing the grass
The gulls circled the pond,
Searching its glazed eye
For the living light,
Remote, still, gold,
And inextricable,
Fading into the halls of cold.

They stood slender with want,
As mobiles of snow
Quivered and sprung
In a flare of wind.
Some hostility unexplained,
Kept me to the window
With empty hands.

And when northward to the coast,
They hung for a moment
In the taut posture of sacrifice,
I felt their cold sea rise against my lips.

FRANCES GILL

GULLS AGROUND

In the green harbour muck, the gulls,
All smooth as sea-pearled mussels, search
For succulent stuff. Strung out in the weed
Some strut, some loll on the slip
And a lone one limps about.
The yearlings croak and the old
Stand round with gossip and laughter,
Lazily sift, or stir their stumps in the rot.
Far off, where the small boats lift,
The sun's edge severs the knot.

When food is found they suddenly have no truck
With each other, but flurrying after,
Will steal, strike, tear or shock
With crude claw or clattering beak
The bird with the luck,
Jerk the crab from its jaw, chop,
Joggle or suck the scrabbling, stark
Shell creature whole into their own maw.

White-eyed they watch for the ones who will come
To throw crumbs and crackling crusts
For the nimble to catch on the air,
Scramble and snatch, give slow, soul-freezing call,
Swoop, slide stiff-legged, tangle again and go
Down to the glimmering slime in a white-fanned fall;
Till the wind-drift turns, the weeds congeal and flow,
The visitors shiver and turn their backs on the dusk
As the tide licks in. Then gulls alight in a row,
Form up and glare like ghosts from the lime-washed wall.

BETTY PARVIN

74

FISH MARKET

Silent, submissive, still,
on antiseptic slabs
the jewelled princes of the sea
were laid. Their names
evoked with breath of brine and drifting sand
the deep, soaked, sea-weed smell
of falling tides. Bream,
dappled plaice and herrings,
Dover sole and squid.

I gazed with sudden tenderness
upon that quiet aristocracy;
exiled from their kingdoms,
fingered, stripped of brightness,
their clean metallic fire destroyed.

And as I dreamed,
a tiny wave slid round my feet,
another and another,
curling wet, tight fingers
round my ankles,
swirling to my knees. And then
through every crack and crevice
the roaring sea came in.
Waves, combed white with shore-winds,
blown to rainbowed foam;
translucent walls of water
beating down from the stalls,
sweeping dust and boxes
out beyond our sight, until
an aqueous, heaving, formless,
glittering flood possessed the world.

The fish, finding their fluid secret ways,
streamed through our minds
into the salt-rippled kingdom of themselves.
For fish evade our touch—

alive or dead, they are intense,
a flash of pure sensation,
surge of liquid fire,
slipping like sparks through our thoughts;
we cannot possess them.
And the sea waits,
waits the moon-drawn moment of awareness
to reclaim us, to engulf us
once again.

RITA PECK

THE TROUT

The trout, speckled and brown and spotted,
White-fleshed, pink-fleshed, rainbow red;
Twisting, darting, sweeping swift
In the chalk stream, rising to bread
Or fly, taking, catching, rejecting, playing
The line. Then down the river, under the alder
A quivering sigh and circle of water,
And peace and a wary peace in the darkling shallows,
Or caught and netted and gutted and colour-dimmed
And still.

MARION MARLOWE

VISION OF THE CUCKOO

Known by the ear; sweet voice, sour reputation;
Seen now and then at distance, the double bell
Dying along your flight; now secretly
From the small window darkened by the yew
I with the eye possess you and your meaning.

Secure you walk, picking your foot under the roses.
The light on the large head is blue,
The wings are netted cinnamon and umber,
The soft dark eye is earthward, the silver belly
Gleams with reflected pink from fallen petals.

I by the world and by myself offended,
Bleeding with outraged love, burning with hate,
Embattled against time my conqueror
In mindbegotten, misbegotten space,
Drink with fierce thirst your drop of absolution.

No love, no hate, no self; only a life,
Blooming in timelessness, in unconceived
Space walking innocent and beautiful;
Guiltless, though myriad-life-devouring;
Guiltless, though tyrant to your fellow-fowls,
You live; and so in me one wound is healed,
Filled with a bright scar, coloured like the roses.

RUTH PITTER

FOR MY LOST NIGHTINGALE

Whoever stole you from that bush of broom,
    I think he envied me my happiness,
O little nightingale, for many a time
    You lightened my sad heart from its distress,
    And flooded my whole soul with melody.
And I would have the other birds all come,
    And sing along with me thy threnody.

So brown and dim that little body was,
    But none could scorn thy singing. In that throat
That tiny throat, what depth of harmony,
    And all night long ringing thy changing note.

What marvel if the cherubim in heaven
Continually do praise Him, when to thee,
O small and happy, such a grace was given?

ALCUIN
(trans. HELEN WADDELL)*
(1889–1965)

LARKS

All day in exquisite air
The song clomb an invisible stair,
Flight on flight, story on story,
Into the dazzling glory.

There was no bird, only a singing,
Up in the glory, climbing and winging,
Like a small golden cloud at even,
Trembling 'twixt earth and heaven.

I saw no staircase, winding, winding,
Up in the dazzle, sapphire and blinding,
Yet round by round, in exquisite air,
The song went up the stair.

KATHERINE TYNAN
(1861–1919)

THE GIFT

I sent my love a little bird,
And sweetly, sweetly did it sing :
It gave him joy and only asked
His cherishing.

He took it from its wooden perch,
And opened wide its tiny beak,
And looked and looked with burning eyes.
It suffered meek.

And then at last he understood
What made the cheerful roundelay.
He was content, but in his hand
A dead bird lay.

ROSAMUND GREENWOOD

SWALLOWS

The swallows pass in restless companies.
Against the pink-flowered may, one shining breast
Throbs momentary music—then, possessed
With motion, sweeps on some new enterprise.
Unquiet in heart, I hear their eager cries
And see them dart to their nests beneath the eaves;
Within my spirit is a voice that grieves,
Reminding me of empty autumn skies.
Nor can we rest in Nature's dear delight :
June droops to winter, and the sun droops west.
Flight is our life. We build our crumbling nest
Beneath the dark eaves of the infinite,
We sing our song in beauty's fading tree,
And flash forth, migrant, into mystery.

MARY WEBB
(1881–1927)

LAUGHTER AND MUSIC

MY HAT

Mother said if I wore this hat
I should be certain to get off with the right sort of chap
Well look where I am now, on a desert island
With so far as I can see no one at all on hand
I know what has happened though I suppose Mother wouldn't
    see
This hat being so strong has completely run away with me
I had the feeling it was beginning to happen the moment I put
    it on
What a moment that was as I rose up, I rose up like a flying
    swan
As strong as a swan too, why see how far my hat has flown me
    away
It took us a night to come and then a night and a day
And all the time the swan wing in my hat waved beautifully
Ah, I thought, How this hat becomes me.
First the sea was dark then it was pale blue
And still the wing beat and we flew and we flew
A night and a day and a night, and by the old right way
Between the sun and the moon we flew until morning day.
It is always early morning here on this peculiar island
The green grass grows into the sea on the dipping land
Am I glad to be here? Yes, well, I am,
It's nice to be rid of Father, Mother and the young man
There's just one thing causes me a twinge of pain,
If I take my hat off, shall I find myself home again?
So in this early morning land I aways wear my hat
Go home, you see, well I wouldn't run a risk like that.

STEVIE SMITH

THE DEDICATED DANCING BULL AND THE WATER MAID

(Beethoven's Sonata in F Op. 17, for Horn and Piano, played by Dennis Brain and Dennis Matthews)

Hop hop, thump thump,
Oh I am holy, oh I am plump,
A young bull dancing on the baked grass glade,
And beside dances the water maid.
She says I must dance with her,
Why should I? I loathe her,
She has such a stupid way of singing
It does not amount to anything,
But she thinks it does, oh yes
She does not suppose she is spurious.
I wish I could be rid of the Water Maid
Or hid from her. Does she think she can make me afraid?
Ho ho, thump thump,
Oh I am elegant, oh I am plump,
As I wave my head my feet go thud
On the baked grass. Oh I am good.
Now night comes and I go into the wood shades
And the moon comes up and lights them as the day fades.

STEVIE SMITH

BALLROOM DANCING CLASS

The little girls' frocks are frilly.
    The little boys' suits are blue.
On little gold chairs
They perch in pairs
    Awaiting their Friday cue.
The little boys stamp like ponies.
    The little girls coo like doves.
The little boys pummel their cronies
    With white enormous gloves.

84

And overhead from a balcony
The twittering mothers crane to see.

Though sleek the curls
Of the little girls,
    Tossing their locks like foam,
Each little boy's tie
Has slipped awry
    And his hair forgets the comb.
He harks to the tuning fiddle
    With supercilious sneers.
His voice is cracked in the middle.
    Peculiar are his ears.
And little girls' mothers nod with poise
To distracted mothers of little boys.

Curtseying to the hostess,
    The little girls dip in line.
But hobbledehoy
Bobs each little boy
    And a ramrod is his spine.
With little girls charms prevailing
    Why, as the music starts,
Are the little girls' mothers paling?
    And why do they clasp their hearts
When the hostess says with an arching glance,
'Let the boys choose partners before we dance'?

Now little girls sway
Like buds in May
    And tremble upon the stalk.
But little boys wear
An arrogant air
    And they swagger when they walk.
The meagerest boy grows taller.
    The shyest one's done with doubt,
As he fingers a manful collar
    And singles his charmer out,

Or rakes the circle with narrowed eyes
To choose his suitable Friday prize.
While overhead in the balcony
The little boys' mothers smile to see
On razorless cheek and beardless chin
The Lord-of-Creation look begin.

Oh, little boys beckon, little girls bend!
And little boys' mothers condescend
(As they straighten their faces and pat their pearls)
To nod to the mothers of little girls.

PHYLLIS MCGINLEY
(U.S.A.)

MAY DAY

Young love in her virginity
Burns up a list of loves,
And runs to meet the latest god
In her best shoes and gloves.
Crying on the silky bedspread
Writing in the dog-eared book,
Hearing her hero at the gate,
Too terrified to look.
The hand of a youth, the light hand
Of a boy that's just left school,
A tentative hand, a white hand
Urgently breaking the rule
With a first embrace and a crushing kiss—
But the girl has hurried away
Sick in her throat and thrilled in her wrists,
With nothing and nothing to say.
With nothing to say and nowhere to go
She dares not lift the cup,

Her wings ungainly weigh her down,
Her feet will trip her up.
She dare not linger by her love
In case her hope is showing,
Nor dare she meet her mother's gaze,
Questioning and knowing.
She dare not stand beside him,
She must be off somewhere,
She drags her wings to the upper deck
and pays a threepenny fare.
She looks back through the coal black glass
And pines to see her man
Look up and wave, oblivious
Of her primordial plan.

He's seventeen and prince of the avenue,
Slave to the world outside,
Inside he lies on a golden bed
And the young girl lies beside—
Beside him dressed in her Sunday best,
They lie and never stir
And she is content to lie by him
And he to lie by her.
And what does the young girl dream of his dreams
Watching him eat his pie,
Assuring her with his mouth full
That he's going to inherit the sky?
What does she know from her scripture—
From Solomon and St. Paul—
Her body erect like a tulip bud,
Short socks beyond recall?
Boys with buns, who whisper bums
And dream of the Golden Fleece—
What does this young girl know of the boy
Waiting for his release?
From a world of broken voices
He'll leap on his dapple grey,
He'll wave to his aunts and uncles
And gallop away,

87

Joyfully riding across the park
Beside the fish-filled lake,
Leaving the gasworks away to the left,
Amazement in his wake.

The boy in the man, the man in the boy,
The creature the young girl fears
Less and less as she sets him free
Over the wedlock years,
The years that burst at every seam,
That rack her tired head,
Sheltering, sewing, feeding, toiling,
Making the long brown bread.
She uses her mind, but the wrap of her womb
Is darkening round her thoughts,
And nothing concludes where she's adding
But rows and rows of noughts :
Egg-like nothings breathing life
Trumpeting into her breast
As she waves to the man who mounts his bicycle
Off on his boyhood quest.
Woman who shudders at harbour and pit
Heavily drenched in black,
Woman who staggers away from the Rising,
Her chattels on her back.
Whatever her teaching, whatever her pitch,
Whatever the stitch of her gloves,
Woman was born to circle the ground
Beneath the man she loves.
Whatever her varnish, her soap, her lies,
Whatever the keys at her side,
Woman was born to open the door
From the inside.

CHARLOTTE MITCHELL

ULTIMATUM

I'm wearied of wearying love, my friend,
    Of worry and strain and doubt;
Before we begin, let us view the end,
    And maybe I'll do without.
There's never the pang that was worth the tear,
    And toss in the night I won't—
So either you do or you don't, my dear,
    Either you do or you don't.

The table is ready, so lay your cards
    And if they should augur pain,
I'll tender you ever my kind regards
    And run for the fastest train.
I haven't the will to be spent and sad;
    My heart's to be gay and true—
Then either you don't or you do, my lad,
    Either you don't or you do!

DOROTHY PARKER
(U.S.A.)
(1893–1967)

THE CHARMING WOMAN

So Miss Myrtle is going to marry?
    What a number of hearts she will break!
There's Lord George, and Tom Brown, and Sir Harry
    Who are dying of love for her sake!
'Tis a match that we all must approve,—
    Let gossips say all that they can!
For indeed she's a charming woman,
    And he's a most fortunate man!

Yes, indeed, she's a charming woman,
    And she reads both Latin and Greek,—

89

And I'm told that she solved a problem
   In Euclid before she could speak!
Had she been but a daughter of mine,
   I'd have taught her to hem and to sew,—
But her mother (a charming woman)
   Couldn't think of such trifles, you know!

Oh, she's really a charming woman!
   But perhaps a little too thin:
And no wonder such very late hours
   Should ruin her beautiful skin!
And her shoulders are rather too bare,
   And her gown's nearly up to her knees,
But I'm told that these charming women
   May dress themselves just as they please!

Yet, she's really a charming woman!
   But I thought I observed, by the bye,
A something—that's rather uncommon,—
   In the flash of that very bright eye?
It may be a mere fancy of mine,
   Tho' her voice has a very sharp tone,—
But I'm told that these charming women
   Are inclined to have wills of their own!

She sings like a bullfinch or linnet,
   And she talks like an Archbishop too;
Can play you a rubber and win it,—
   If she's got nothing better to do!
She can chatter of Poor-Laws and Tithes,
   And the value of labour and land,—
'Tis a pity when charming women
   Talk of things which they don't understand!

I'm told that she hasn't a penny,
   Yet her gowns would make Maradan stare;
And I feel her bills must be many,—
   But that's only her husband's affair!
Such husbands are very uncommon,
   So regardless of prudence and pelf,—

But they say such a charming woman
  Is a fortune, you know, in herself.

She's brothers and sisters by dozens,
  And all charming people, they say !
And several tall Irish cousins
  Whom she loves in a sisterly way.
O young men, if you'd take my advice,
  You would find it an excellent plan,—
Don't marry a charming woman,
  If you are a sensible man.

HELEN SELINA (LADY DUFFERIN)
(1807–1867)

FRESHMEN

(With apologies to Masefield)

    Scholar-type from Winchester or (sometimes) Eton
    Coming up to New Coll with other pleasant guys,
    With luggage full of Berlioz,
    Lapsang Soochong,
    Apparatus criticus and neat, bow ties.

    Mustard-keen commoner from Midland grammar school,
    Never letting on he doesn't know the ropes,
    With luggage full of Salad Days
    Penguins, County Grants,
    Sherry glasses, marmalade and microscopes.

    Muscle-man from Empire with dirt-caked sports shorts,
    Butting through the trials to an Oxford Blue,
    With luggage full of Tiger Rag,
    Food stuffs, track-suits,
    Liniment, boots and a book, or two.

MAIDA STANIER

HIAWATHA'S PANCAKE

(Oxford's first Shrove Tuesday Pancake Race was run in Christ Church Meadows to the strains of trombone, clarinet and double-bass. It was won by a psychologist from Harvard who smoked a cigar throughout.)

Should you ask me whence those stories,
Whence those legends and traditions
That are told concerning Oxford
By the old man after dinner,
Over port and after dinner,
I should answer, lucky readers
You are in at the beginning
Of a legend just created.
For on Tuesday, Pancake Tuesday,
All the braves in Oxford gathered
To behold the pancake-tossers
Run their race through Christ Church meadow,
To the pounding of the tom-tom,
Clarinet and contra-basso
Run their first race through the Meadow.
Chief among them ran the Yan-kee,
Mighty medicine man of Harvard,
With cigar made heap big magic
To defeat his fellow-runners
With a sense of his importance.
Cunningly he lagged behind them,
Cunningly he tossed his pancake,
Smiled to see the bits of gravel
Sticking to his rivals' pancake
To the oft-misfielded pancake,
Laughed to see them try to eat it,
Laughed to see them spit out gravel,
'Ugh!' they said and spat out gravel.
Then the Yan-kee drawing level,
His Corona for the moment
Laid aside and scoffed the pancake
In one mighty mastication.

As the whale engulfs the plankton
So he scoffed his nice clean pancake.
As the arrow to the target
So he sped towards the finish,
So he flashed towards the finish
And they all declared him winner
Of the First Great Pancake Contest.
And when back again to Harvard
To his wigwam he betakes him
He will say to his papooses,
'Should you ask me whence those stories,
Whence those legends and traditions . . .'

MAIDA   STANIER

PICTURES

The Toulouse-Lautrec woman
Lolls with open mouth
Round rakish hat, striped skirt,
Hands fierce as agaves
Aslant the hotel balcony—
While miniature below
Some dolls of children play with neat mammas
Crisp-washed
In Boudin domesticity
Beside a docile pearly-tinted sea.

In the harbour
A boat by Derain
Breaks the pale sky with harsh, erratic sails,
Sharpens deep shadows under prow and stern.
Behind her, dizzy, buzzing with the blues
And greens of shimmering sea and white ecstatic rigging
Yachts from the regatta idle in
Painted by Dufy from an open window.

While down the street
In starched and prim stiff skirt
A small girl walks unconscious of the summer,
The sea, the boats, the harbour—
Her eyes upon the painter, Renoir,
Drawing her into immortality,
Drawing her sand-soft hair, her sea-blue pinafore,
Straw hat and limpid gloves
And mussel-shining shoes.

SYLVIA READ

FULL MOON

She was wearing the coral taffeta trousers
Some one had brought her from Isphahan
And the little gold coat with pomegranate blossoms
And the coral-hafted feather fan;
And she ran down a Kentish lane in the moonlight
And skipped in the pool of the moon as she ran.

She cared not a rap for all the big planets,
For Betelgeuse or Aldebaran
And all the big planets cared nothing for her—
That small impertinent charlatan;
But she climbed on a Kentish stile in the moolight
And laughed at the sky through the sticks of her fan!

VICTORIA SACKVILLE-WEST
(1892–1962)

THE GIRL WITH THE BALL

She ran with her ball in her light dress floating and free
Tossing it, tossing it up in the evening light.
She ran with her ball at the edge of the outgoing sea
On sand which the dropping sun turned bright.

94

Over the sea hung birds more white than the skin
Of the last few swimmers who took the waves with their breasts.
The birds dipped straight as her ball when a silver fin
Glanced in the shallow crests.

She ran so swift, and suddenly stopped as swift
To look at a shell or splash up a pool in rain.
Wind blew, and she in the wind began to drift
Foam-like and suddenly ran again.

Children who played on the shore in the last of the day
Paused to watch in wonder her rise and fall
Like elders watching a child : she was younger than they
As she ran by the sea with her ball.

Her hair was loose and she had no shoes on her feet
And her image ran under her feet on the wet gold shore.
She threw up her ball and caught it and once laughed sweet
As though the world had never heard laughter before.

ELEANOR FARJEON
(1887–1965)

'I TASTE A LIQUOR NEVER BREWED'

I taste a liquor never brewed,
From tankards scooped in pearl;
Not all the vats upon the Rhine
Yield such an alcohol!

Inebriate of air am I,
And debauchee of dew,
Reeling, through endless summer days,
From inns of molten blue.

When landlords turn the drunken bee
Out of the foxglove's door,
When butterflies renounce their drams,
I shall but drink the more!

Till seraphs swing their snowy hats,
And saints to windows run,
To see the little tippler
Leaning against the sun!

EMILY DICKINSON*
(U.S.A.)
(1850–1886)

HEART AND MIND

Said the Lion to the Lioness—'When you are amber dust,—
No more a raging fire like the heat of the Sun
(No liking but all lust)—
Remember still the flowering of the amber blood and bone
The rippling of bright muscles like a sea,
Remember the rose-prickles of bright paws
Though we shall mate no more
Till the fire of that sun the heart and the moon-cold bone are
    one.'

Said the Skeleton lying upon the sands of Time—
'The great gold planet that is the mourning heat of the Sun
Is greater than all gold, more powerful
Than the tawny body of a Lion that fire consumes
Like all that grows or leaps . . . so is the heart
More powerful than all dust. Once I was Hercules
Or Samson, strong as the pillars of the seas :
But the flames of the heart consumed me, and the mind
Is but a foolish wind.'

96

Said the Sun to the Moon—'When you are but a lonely white
   crone,
And I, a dead King in my golden armour somewhere in a dark
   wood,
Remember only this of our hopeless love
That never till Time is done
Will the fire of the heart and the fire of the mind be one.'

EDITH SITWELL
(1887–1964)

THE SWANS

In the green light of water, like the day
Under green boughs, the spray
And air-pale petals of the foam seem flowers,—
Dark-leaved arbutus blooms with wax-pale bells
And their faint honey-smells,
The velvety syringa with smooth leaves,
Gloxinia with a green shade in the snow,
Jasmine and moon-clear orange-blossoms and green blooms
Of the wild strawberries from the shade of woods.
Their showers
Pelt the white women under the green trees,
Venusia, Cosmopolita, Pistillarine—
White solar statues, white rose-trees in snow
Flowering for ever, child-women, half stars
Half flowers, waves of the sea, born of a dream.

Their laughter flying through the trees like doves,
These angels come to watch their whiter ghosts
In the air-pale water, archipelagos
Of stars and young thin moons from great wings falling
As ripples widen.
These are their ghosts, their own white angels these!

O great wings spreading—
Your bones are made of amber, smooth and thin
Grown from the amber dust that was a rose
Or nymph in swan-smooth waters.
                              But time's winter falls
With snows as soft, as soundless . . . Then, who knows
Rose-footed swan from snow, or girl from rose?

                                        EDITH SITWELL
                                        (1887–1964)

GLORIA IN EXCELSIS
Clouds over Yew

          Fold your impetuous hands and kneel
          On crowding daisies furred in dew,
          And with their innocence look up
          Between the tall flames of the yew
          To where the white, imperial clouds
          Sojurn awhile, divinely slow,
        Like swans that sleep upon illustrious water
        Breasting the warm air with a shield of snow.

                                        JILL FURSE*
                                        (1915–1944)

THE HARE IS VANISHED

          The hare is vanished from the darkening hill,
          Colour from beauty, and the heart is still.
          The lark no longer from his spiral stair
          Exhorts the shepherd in the sunlit air.

Now along silent lanes a shower is born
In unlit diamonds on the margin thorn,
And on the mournful gate a fringe of tears
Delays to weep until the moon appears.
Now one by one within the valley's fold
Infrequent windows open eyes of gold,
And pause unwinking in the falling rain,
Or edge in envy round the patient train
That through the small and fading landscape plies
Like a bright needle in old tapestries.

JILL FURSE*
(1915–1944)

POSSESSION

Thou hast no grave. What is it that bereaves,
That has bereft us of thee? Thou art gone!
The forest with its infinite soft leaves
May have received thee, or thou wandered'st on,
The tender, wild, exhilarating flowers
Crowning thy broken pathway; or the white
Glare of the torrent smote thee; or the powers
Of the great sculptured country, from their height
Prompted thee upward. Thou hast made no plea
For rest or for possession; and thy hold
Is on the land forever : thine the gold
Brimming the crystal crests, the gold that fills
The vales, the valley's purity,
And thine the inmost meadows of the hills.

'MICHAEL FIELD'*
(1846–1914)
(1862–1913)

99

THE CRYSTAL TREE

Not with my thoughts shall you be weighted
My lovely, delicate crystal tree,
You shall be clear and separated
From the unresting soul in me.

You shall not with my breath be misted
Or with my touch grow undefined;
You shall not be wrenched out and twisted
To fill the crannies of my mind.

You shall not shake beneath the thunder,
Suffer the tempest's disarray;
You shall grow timelessly in wonder
Who are not rooted in the clay.

The heart that, desperate and lawless,
Clutches at joy, shall leave you free;
You shall shine on, unchanged and flawless,
My lovely, delicate crystal tree.

PHYLLIS MÉGROZ

THE UNICORN

Hate me or love, I care not, as I pass
To those hid citadels
Where in the depth of my enchanted glass
The changeless image dwells;
To where for ever blooms the nameless tree;
For ever, alone and fair,
The lovely Unicorn beside the sea
Is laid, and slumbers there.

Give or withhold, all's nothing, as I go
On to those glimmering grounds

Where falling secretly and quiet as snow
The silent music sounds;
Where earth is withered away before the eyes,
And heaven hangs in the air,
For in the oak the bird of paradise
Alights, and triumphs there.

Slay me or spare, it matters not : I fly
Ever, for ever rest
Alone and with a host : in the void sky
There do I build my nest :
I lay my beams from star to star, and make
My house where all is bare;
Hate, slay, withhold, I rear it for thy sake
And thou art with me there.

RUTH PITTER

EURYDICE

In a green woodland,
    Beneath a slender tree,
All the bright morning
    Sleeps Eurydice.

'Make my bed narrow,
    And dig my grave deep,
For I shall not awaken
    The next time I sleep.'

'Have no doubt, lady,
    You shall awake :
Dead men and demons
    Shall dance for your sake.'

Who shall tell
   Of the banquet spread,
The spellbound king,
   And the rustling dead;

The whirling dance
   And the wished word spoken,
The promise made
   And the promise broken?

In a green woodland,
   Beside a grey stone,
All the bright morning
   Sits Orpheus alone.

Sweetly, and sadly,
   And merrily plays he,
The dog-fox leaves the bracken
   And rubs against his knee;

The harp-notes hang like willow leaves
   Upon the slender tree,
But no song will ever
   Wake Eurydice.

DOROTHY HOWARD

FAIRY-LED

The fairy people flouted me,
Mocked me, shouted me—
They chased me down the dreamy hill and beat me with a
   wand
Within the wood they found me, put spells on me and bound
   me
And left me at the edge of day in John the miller's pond.

Beneath the eerie starlight
Their hair shone curd-white;
Their bodies were all twisted like a lichened apple-tree;
Feather-light and swift they moved,
And never one the other loved,
For all were full of ancient dreams and dark designs on me.

With noise of leafy singing
And white wands swinging,
They marched away amid the grass that swayed to let them
    through.
Between the yellow tansies
Their eyes, like purple pansies,
Peered back on me before they passed all trackless in the dew.

MARY WEBB
(1881–1927)

AZAY-LE-RIDEAU
At the Chateau

What lutes, what notes, what waterfalls of music,
Voices of summer dying on the wind;
From the carved balustrades, the formal gardens
The murmuring laughter eddies to its end.
Over the paving-stones the lingering crimson,
Linden and gold, a burden of brocade;
In the stitched meadows of a thousand flowers
Pensive as listeners to a silent music
They dream, enchanted, in the close-leaved shade.

Oh idle hands beneath the falling fountain,
Gloved fingers resting on the marble urn,
Hands that withdraw, that speak, that lie together
Folded like wings upon a shaft of stone.
Distant as figures dancing in a landscape

103

This fabled grace gives back its youth to Age,
Prisoned and held upon a web of canvas
Or shut forever in a Book of Hours
Between the enamelled and the gilded page.

ROSEMARY DOBSON
(Australia)

GLAMOUR

The linnet is here, and the lark, and the yellowhammer
And the thrush that sings so clear at the break of day.
The small brown birds are here : but the bright bird Glamour
Has opened his shining wings and flown away.
He lit on my hand for a while—I heard his singing
That was like an ache and a flame, a dream and a star;
But now the sound grows faint; I can see him singing
Through the dark woods of the world, travelling far.

It is he that young men dare for and old men sigh for,
It is he that calls the sailors down to the sea,
It is he that women bear for and soldiers die for,
And where he has been comfort no more shall be.
Through the dark woods of the world I stumble on :
'Glamour, O bright bird Glamour, where have you gone?'

JAN STRUTHER

ASPECTS OF LOVE

SELF AND THE OTHERSELF

I grieve; and dare not show my discontent!
I love; and yet am forced to seem to hate!
I do; yet dare not say, I ever meant!
I seem stark mute; but inwardly do prate!
I am, and not; I freeze and yet am burned;
Since from myself, my otherself I turned!

My care is like my shadow in the sun;
Follows me flying! flies, when I pursue it!
Stands and lies by me! doth what I have done!
This too familiar Care doth make me rue it!
Nor means I find, to rid him from my breast,
Till, by the end of things, it be supprest.

Some gentler Passions slide into my mind;
For I am soft, and made of melting snow.
Or be more cruel, Love! and so be kind :
Let me, or float, or sink! be high, or low!
Or let me live with some more sweet content;
Or die! and so forget what Love e'er meant.

QUEEN ELIZABETH I
(1533–1603)

SCENE AT EVENING

This is the image : the forsaken street
with one clear doorway where the figure stands :
gathering with unpractised hands
the last receding sound of feet.

Like a fruit, ripened, falls the night
now the sun is gone, The still, chill air
wears a pattern of jewels like a fair.
The wet stones mirror lacquered light.

107

Like a bell, the shell of the sky is cast
with a voice rending the past with a cry
as the ear of the night is riven by
a train's abandoned whistle-blast.

The theme is constant : they are bound to part :
he on a quest that no woman may share
while she must remain waiting there
housing the roots of his life in her heart.

KAREN GERSHON

TO AUSONIUS

I, through all chances that are given to mortals,
  And through all fates that be,
So long as this close prison shall contain me,
  Yea, though a world shall sunder me and thee,

Thee shall I hold, in every fibre woven,
  Not with dumb lips, nor with averted face
Shall I behold thee, in my mind embrace thee,
  Instant and present, thou, in every place.

Yea, when the prison of this flesh is broken,
  And from the earth I shall have gone my way,
Whersoe'er in the wide universe I stay me,
  There shall I bear thee, as I do today.

Think not the end, that from my body frees me,
  Breaks and unshackles from my love to thee;
Triumphs the soul above its house in ruin,
  Deathless, begot of immortality.

Still must she keep her senses and affections,
   Hold them as dear as life itself to be.
Could she choose death, then might she choose forgetting :
   Living, remembering, to eternity.

PAULINUS OF NOLA
(trans. HELEN WADDELL)*
(1889–1965)

AND ON MY EYES DARK SLEEP BY NIGHT

Come, dark-eyed Sleep, thou child of Night,
Give me thy dreams, thy lies;
Lead through the horny portal white
The pleasure day denies.

O bring the kiss I could not take
From lips that would not give;
Bring me the heart I could not break,
The bliss for which I live.

I care not if I slumber blest
By fond delusion; nay,
Put me on Phaon's lips to rest,
And cheat the cruel day !

'MICHAEL FIELD'*
(1846–1914)
(1862–1913)

SECOND THOUGHTS

I thought of leaving her for a day
In town, it was such iron winter
At Durdans, the garden frosty clay,
The woods as dry as any splinter,
The sky congested. I would break
From the deep, lethargic, country air
To the shining lamps, to the clash of the play,
And to-morrow, wake
Beside her, a thousand things to say.
I planned—O more—I had almost started;—
I lifted her face in my hands to kiss,—
A face in a border of fox's fur,
For the bitter black wind had stricken her,
And she wore it—her soft hair straying out
Where it buttoned against the gray, leather snout:
In an instant we should have parted;
But at sight of the delicate world within
That fox-fur collar, from brow to chin,
At sight of those wonderful eyes from the mine,
Coal pupils, an iris of glittering spa,
And the wild, ironic, defiant shine
As of a creature behind a bar
One has captured, and, when three lives are past,
May hope to reach the heart of at last,
All that, and the love at her lips, combined
To shew me what folly it were to miss
A face with such thousand things to say,
And beside these, such thousand more to spare,
For the shining lamps, for the clash of the play—
O madness; not for a single day
Could I leave her! I stayed behind.

'MICHAEL FIELD'*
(1846–1914)
(1862–1913)

SONG

As the inamour'd Thirsis lay
  With his Sylvia reconcil'd,
Whose eyes did brighter beams display,
  While the lovely charmer smil'd,

With joy transported, cry'd my dear,
  Let us, let us, often jar,
Peace always sweetest does appear
  After sharp fatigues of war.

No, said the nymph, mistaken swain,
  'Tis best our quarrels to give o'er;
Kingdoms may jar and close again
  But broken love cements no more.

APHRA BEHN*
(1640–1689)

A LETTER TO HER HUSBAND,
ABSENT UPON PUBLICK EMPLOYMENT

As loving Hind that (Hartless) wants her Deer,
Scuds through the woods and fern with harkning ear,
Perplext, in every bush and nook doth pry
Her dearest Deer might answer ear or eye :
So doth my anxious soul, which now doth miss
A dearer Dear (far dearer Heart) than this,
Still wait with doubts, and hopes, and failing eye,
His voice to hear or person to discry.
Or as the pensive Dove doth all alone
On withered bough most uncouthly bemoan
The absence of her Love and loving Mate,
Whose loss hath made her so unfortunate :
Ev'n thus doe I, with many a deep sad groan,
Bewail my turtle true, who now is gone,

111

His presence and his safe return still woo
With thousand dolefull sighs and mournfull Coo.
Or as the loving Mullet, that true Fish
Her fellow lost, nor joy nor life doth wish,
But lanches on that shore, there for to dye
Where she her captive husband doth espy.
Mine being gone, I lead a joyless life,
I have a loving fere, yet seem no wife :
But worst of all, to him can't steer my course,
I here, he there, alas, both kept by force.
Return my Dear, my joy, my only Love,
Unto thy Hinde, thy Mullet and thy Dove,
Who neither joyes in pasture, house nor streams;
The substance gone, O me, these are but dreams.
Together at one Tree, oh let us brouze,
And like two Turtles roost within one house,
And like the Mullets in one River glide,
Let's still remain but one, till death divide.
        Thy loving Love and Dearest Dear,
        At home, abroad, and everywhere.

ANNE BRADSTREET*
(U.S.A.)
(1612–1672)

TO LYSANDER

(On some verses he writ, and asking more for his heart than it was worth.)

    Take back the heart you with such caution give,
      Take the fond valu'd trifle back :
    I hate love merchants that a trade wou'd drive
      And meanly cunning bargains make.

    I care not how the busy market goes
      And scorn to chaffer for a price :

Love does one staple rate on all impose,
  Nor leaves it to the trader's choice.

A heart requires a heart unfeign'd and true,
  Though subtly you advance the price;
And ask a rate that simple love ne'er knew
  And the free trade monopolize.

An humble slave the buyer must become,
  She must not bate a look or glance
You will have all or you'll have none;
  See how love's market you inhance.

It's not enough I gave you heart for heart,
  But I must add my lips and eyes;
I must no smile or friendly kiss impart;
  But you must dun me with advice . . .

Be just, my lovely swain, and do not take
  Freedoms you'll not to me allow :
O give Aminta so much freedom back
  That she may rove as well as you.

Let us then love upon the honest square
  Since interest neither have design'd,
For the sly gamester, who ne'er plays me fair
  Must trick for trick expect to find.

APHRA BEHN*
(1640–1689)

I DO NOT LOVE THEE

I do not love thee ! No ! I do not love thee !
And yet when thou art absent I am sad;
And envy even the bright blue sky above thee,
Whose quiet stars may see thee and be glad.

113

I do not love thee! yet, I know not why,
Whate'er thou dost seems still well done, to me—
And often in my solitude I sigh—
That those I *do* love are not more like thee!

I do not love thee! yet, when thou art gone
I hate the sound (though those who speak be dear)
Which breaks the lingering echo of the tone
Thy voice of music leaves upon my ear.

I do not love thee! yet thy speaking eyes,
With their deep, bright and most expressive blue—
Between me and the midnight heaven arise,
Oftener than any eyes I ever knew.

I *know* I do not love thee! yet, alas!
Others will scarcely trust my candid heart;
And oft I catch them smiling as they pass,
Because they see me gazing where thou art.

CAROLINE NORTON*
(1808–1876)

MY MOTHER BIDS ME BIND MY HAIR

My mother bids me bind my hair
With bands of rosy hue,
Tie up my sleeves with ribbons rare,
And lace my bodice blue.

For why, she cries, sit still and weep,
While others dance and play?
Alas! I scarce can go or creep
While Lubin is away.

'Tis sad to think the days are gone
When those we love were near;
I sit upon this mossy stone
And sigh when none can hear.

And while I spin my flaxen thread
And sing my simple lay,
The village seems asleep, or dead,
Now Lubin is away.

MRS. JOHN HUNTER
(Scotland)
(dates untraced)

A BUD IN THE FROST

Blow on the embers, an' sigh at the sparkles!
My mother she bid me be wise in time.—
Ashes are white an' the red fires darkles;
I lost the words, but I know the rhyme.

It may be true
An' it may be true,
'Tis much to me, 'tis little to you!
Oh, look if a boat comes over the water,
An' call on my mother who told her daughter
That "Love is all crost,—like a bud in the frost."

Love has undone me, an' why would you wonder!
My mother she bid me be wise in time.—
The waters have met, an' my head has gone under,
But far, far away there are bells that chime
How love is no liar,
Oh, love is no liar.
"That's only a bird singin' there on the briar.

115

You'd better be lookin' no more at the water
But give me your hand an' come home, my daughter,
For love is all crost,—like a bud in the frost."

MOIRA O'NEILL
(Ireland)
(1874–1965)

DICHOTOMY

The fairy tales were right and they were wrong,
The Princess always found her perfect Prince,
And happy ever after was the song
We learnt as children and have wanted since.
A hedge of thorn was powerless to keep
The ardent bridegroom from the ardent bride,
A hundred years was not too long to sleep
For love triumphant would not be denied.
But life does not possess this magic charm,
And men and women lack a binding spell,
And likenesses so different feed alarm,
And each in isolation fathoms hell.
Rapunzel can't let down her lovely hair,
The ivory tower stays without a stair.

HELEN FORSYTH
(Scotland)

THE PRICE OF LOVE

Sharp, double-edged and gleaming like a sword
Our joy will pierce us to the heart each night.
To cheat the fear that lurks in our delight
We'll guard with jealous care our precious hoard:

Those tender moments, quiet in their bliss
When thought runs to meet thought, and on the swift
Impact, the spirit quickens to uplift
Its wings in flight, and everything to this
Seems immaterial and subordinate.
We will not rail at time and call him 'thief';
Nor will we count a single minute brief
That yields us moments such as these; nor rate
The price of love exorbitant, if death
Or pain extinguishes its vital breath.

MURIEL BOX

LAMENT OF HELOISE

No second spring can melt this winter-sadness
And break again in such brave buds of light.
Nor birds sing now with the old poignant gladness
Of Breton mornings, when the bloom fell white
On orchard grass, and my young blood was burning
For Abelard the proud, whose eagle mind
Reached down a star to read by : in that learning
And love alone my soul its truth could find.

The vesper bell fills these still cloister shadows,
Dim burns the candle here at Argenteuil;
Relentlessly each leafless year will come,
Falling like snow on memory's April meadows :
Since for our sin God took my love away
The singing birds within my heart are dumb.

MARGARET WILLY

from MADELEINE IN CHURCH

How old was Mary out of whom you cast
So many devils? Was she young or perhaps for years
She had sat staring, with dry eyes, at this and that man going
    past
Till suddenly she saw You on the steps of Simon's house
And stood and looked at You through tears.
    I think she must have known by those
The thing, for what it was that had come to her.
For some of us there is a passion, I suppose
So far from earthly cares and earthly fears
That in its stillness you can hardly stir,
    Or in its nearness lift your hand,
So great that you have simply got to stand
Looking at it through tears, through tears;
    Then straight from these there broke the kiss.
    I think You must have known by this
The thing, for what it was, that had come to You :
    She did not love You like the rest,
It was in her own way, but at the worst, the best.
    She gave you something altogether new.
And through it all, from her no word,
She scarcely saw You, scarcely heard :
Surely you knew when she so touched You with her hair,
    Or by the wet cheek lying there,
And while her perfume clung to You from head to foot all
    through the day
That You can change the things for which we care,
But, even You, unless You kill us, not the way.

This, then, was peace for her, but passion too.
I wonder was it like a kiss that once I knew,
    The only one that I would care to take
Into the grave with me, to which if there were afterwards, to
    wake.
    Almost as happy as the carven dead
In some dim chancel lying head by head
We slept with it, but face to face, the whole night through—

118

One breath, one throbbing quietness, as if the thing behind
  our lips was endless life,
Lost, as I woke, to hear in the strange earthly dawn, his
  "Are you there?"
And lie still, listening to the wind outside, among the firs.
So Mary chose the dream of Him for what was left to her
  of night and day.
It is the only truth; it is the dream in us that neither life
  nor death nor any other thing can take away :
But if she had not touched Him in the doorway of the
  dream could she have cared so much?
She was a sinner, we are what we are : the spirit after-
  wards, but first the touch.

CHARLOTTE MEW*
(1869–1928)

SYMPATHY

His pains so racked my heart
  That soon I had forgot
Whether in him or me they had their start.
  And though I had no lot
  In griefs that him abused
  I thought one day, confused,
If I should cease to feel, O God what gain !
  An end to all his pain.

VIOLA MEYNELL
(1888–1956)

REGRETS

As, when the seaward ebbing tide doth pour
  Out by the low sand spaces,
The parting waves slip back to clasp the shore
  With lingering embraces,—

119

So, in the tide of life that carries me
    From where thy true heart dwells,
Waves of my thoughts and memories turn to thee
    With lessening farewells;

Waving of hands; dreams, when the day forgets;
    A care half lost in cares;
The saddest of my verses; dim regrets;
    Thy name among my prayers.

I would the day might come, so waited for,
    So patiently besought,
When I returning, should fill up once more
    Thy desolated thought;

And fill thy loneliness that lies apart
    In still, persistent pain.
Shall I content thee, O thou broken heart,
    As the tide comes again,

And brims the little sea-shore lakes, and sets
    Seaweeds afloat, and fills
The silent pools, rivers and rivulets
    Among the inland hills?

ALICE MEYNELL
(1847–1922)

EPITAPH

I recreate you out of light and shadow,
Red leaf, blue feather, winter silences
Where snow and wood-smoke weave your words together
For frost to hammer into singing trees.

Not in such rooms as we must still inhabit
Will you be found again, but in that glen
Between the warm rock and the witch-dark water,
Striding a ridge undared by other men.

You were not made for age to disinherit;
Unleased to Death your spirit travels free
Beyond our mundane reach, yet turn one minute
And look into my eyes until I see
Myself re-born in yours, and your reflection
Flashed on the glass dividing you and me.

Breath, do not blur these fragments while I gather
Full store for memory to feed upon;
I build your image through unfaithful weather
That would betray me, finding you are gone.
Gone where? Gone nowhere while I climb towards you
And carve your name on water, earth, and air
Till letting go the rope that will not hold you,
I fall back in the dark—and you are there.

PHOEBE HESKETH

RESCUE

Into my green and greedy lap you poured
Treasures more fit for gods than men to hold;
Out of my mouth and eyes such promise soared
To fall like a frozen bird at the touch of cold.

As the trusting Falconer sets loose his bird
In dare-deep azure from the safety-green,
You gave me liberty with loving word;
But the beckoning world swelled apple-red between
Your loving and my living; cloud and leaf
Disguised my actions, muted your command.
Hot seasons melted will, untied belief
Till resolutions ran like running sand.

And I was running, flying from my Lover,
Pursuing crooked loves with subtle lies;

121

Giving what was not mine, I sought to cover
Betrayal with a benefactor's guise.

I touched delight that vanished at my grasping;
Each fruit I reached for trapped me in its briar;
Through the wilderness you waited on my asking
For rescue from air-pockets of desire.

Now I alighting on your outstretched hand,
Return my head to that once-hated hood—
It gives me sight, revealing sky and land
Long hidden for your purpose and my good.

Thus chained and hooded, I am free at last
Exploring unknown kingdoms of the mind;
Shipwrecked from my self, I see a mast
Grown in the woods of home I left behind.

PHOEBE HESKETH

SPEEDING SHIP

Steer me my splendid ship
Of memory, your sails unfurled
Enough to take the whip
Of tides across the world.

Steer me my lonely barque
Of memory into the night's
Deep and protective dark—
Chasing receding light.

Steer me my cunning craft
Of memory and land my mind
Shipwrecked upon the raft
Of loving left behind.

122

Steer me, winged memory
My friend, my bitter bitter friend,
   And spin eternity
Into my time—and after's end.

ERICA MARX

STORY OF A HOTEL ROOM

Thinking we were safe—insanity !
We went in to make love. All the same
Idiots to trust the little hotel bedroom.
Then in the gloom . . .
 . . . And who does not know that pair of shutters
With the awkward hook on them
All screeching whispers ? Very well then, in the gloom
We set about acquiring one another
Urgently ! But on a temporary basis
Only as guests—just guests of one another's senses.

But idiots to feel so safe you hold back nothing
Because the bed of cold, electric linen
Happens to be illicit . . .
To make love as well as that is ruinous.
Londoner, Parisian, someone should have warned us
That without permanent intentions
You have absolutely no protection
—If the act is clean, authentic, sumptuous,
The concurring deep love of the heart
Follows the naked work, profoundly moved by it.

ROSEMARY TONKS

TIGERS

I try not to write about tigers,
But when I try to write about us
On they come, their smooth coats rippling with
Light, their eyes fixed on the horizon.
They do not look at us; they do not
Greet us as their cousins. Why should we
Imagine that we resemble them?

We do not, in fact, fight like tigers.
Look, the cubs are only playing : you
Would think their teeth made of rubber, and
Their pretty claws. We hurt. We draw blood.
The grown ones, too, do not fight. We may
See them gliding out softly, at night,
Together. They are going to kill
Something else : not to hurt each other.
Why should they tear gold and black striped fur,
Gulp tigers' blood? They have other prey.
We must admire their common sense.

This
Is the first lesson from tigers.
Then there is the lesson of patience,
And the lesson of watchfulness. Look
At their eyes—golden, unblinking, sure.
Our eyes are grey, with a tawny ring
Around the pupil, like a circle
Of fur : identical, yours with mine.
(We think we understand what this means :
We are too alike, we say.) Tigers
Do not use their eyes on each other
As weapons—nor in these long sucking
Glances, that hold us together, drained
Of breath. Tigers are above such things.

These tigers will have to go. They are
A distraction. There is one thing, though,

124

That I should like to tell them : Listen,
Tigers, I would say : you think you know
All you need—burning, as the man said,
In your forests; but we could teach you.
They would listen remotely, as I
Tried to describe for them a matter
In which we approach them : there is a
Felinity in our best actions.
But what else there is in our loving
They cannot know, nor can I tell them.
Let them go, then, uncomprehending.
If they could understand even they,
The proud tigers, might be envious.

FLEUR ADCOCK
(New Zealand)

NOCTURNS AND MEDITATIONS

THE NIGHT-LIGHT

Outside the study door the candles wait,
Ranged in a row, respectable, sedate.
Snuffers in front of each, like hats in church
Devoutly set before each worshipper.
First father's candlestick which bears upright
A virgin wick, untouched, new every night.
The silver stand, guiltless of finger smirch
Shines brightly as a well-soaped chorister.

My mother's next, old-fashioned, square it stands
A little crookt. So many tired hands
With loosened hold have tilted it askew
And dulled the brass with scattered waxen tears.
The visitors have coloured china ware
Sprigged over with small flowers. The servants share
Humble enamel, chipped, and ringed with blue.
No candle waits to comfort my night fears,

For in this house, where blessed love is blind
They think me still a child, and I shall find
Awaiting me in my low room upstairs
A night-light vigilant beside my bed.
With paper girt, borne on a saucered sea
It lifts a golden circle steadfastly,
And when I say my half-remembered prayers
Haloes with light my bowed, unworthy head.

BARBARA VERE HODGE

ON A PICTURE BY SMITH HALDY

A full moon lamps it in a cloudless sky,
And boats, high-prowed, lie black against the path
Of radiance, across a tideless sea.

129

The strand is black with footsteps in the snow.
No soul in sight. And yet my fancy hears
That clear, unearthly, and enchanting ring
Which voices, heard across the snow, can bring.

It seems a land-locked sea. The Ijsselmeer?
And yet—can it indeed be truly Dutch,
With their meticulous domestic touch?
For look—an open window overhead,
And there, across the window-sill outspread
Forgotten lies the housewife's feather-bed!

ALICE ALMENT

FLOWERING CURRANT

Into this city room your pungent scent
Has brought the ghosts of shy forgotten springs;
Dim April dusks, that linger still and make
The daffodils dance wanly in their rings.
You are Alladin's lamp, for when I rub
Your wrinkled leaves and press them to my face
Here is another spell; the spring has gone
And candle light has come to take its place.
A child sits up in bed, the curtain shakes
While down the chimney roars the winter storm.
Someone comes in and brings black-currant tea:
The world has grown sweet-scented, safe and warm.

EILUNED LEWIS
(Wales)

THE MOON AND THE YEW TREE

This is the light of the mind, cold and planetary.
The trees of the mind are black. The light is blue.
The grasses unload their griefs on my feet as if I were God,
Prickling my ankles and murmuring of their humility.
Fumey, spiritous mists inhabit this place
Separated from my house by a row of headstones.
I simply cannot see where there is to get to.

The moon is no door. It is a face in its own right,
White as a knuckle and terribly upset.
It drags the sea after it like a dark crime; it is quiet
With the O-gape of complete despair. I live here.
Twice on Sunday, the bells startle the sky—
Eight great tongues affirming the Resurrection.
At the end, they soberly bong out their names.

The yew tree points up. It has a Gothic shape.
The eyes lift after it and find the moon.
The moon is my mother. She is not sweet like Mary.
Her blue garments unloose small bats and owls.
How I would like to believe in tenderness—
The face of the effigy, gentled by candles,
Bending, on me in particular, its mild eyes.

I have fallen a long way. Clouds are flowering
Blue and mystical over the face of the stars.
Inside the church, the saints will be all blue,
Floating on their delicate feet over the cold pews,
Their hands and faces stiff with holiness.
The moon sees nothing of this. She is bald and wild.
And the message of the yew tree is blackness—blackness and
   silence.

SYLVIA PLATH*
(U.S.A.)
(1932–1963)

131

ST. MARKS, MIDNIGHT

I

Like a ballooning pavilion with lances pinned down,
Haunted and hunched in her gorgeous, her tarnishing dreams,
She broods there, the ancient, the Eastern one, moon of the seas.
A downpour has polished the paving and God in the wings
Has shaken his thundersheet, flourished his lightnings about,
Scattering loiterers, sweeping the marble stage bare
Of all but the tables and chairs and a lighted string band,
The waltz music hollowly swirling in dim colonnades.

II

Enter the Old Count
and the Jilted Lady,
no strangers to the game.
She tells her grief,
he names a famous name
and speaks of love
foregone for honour's sake.
He buys her flowers
and still the strings play on.
He lends his arm,
escorts her to her door.
'Passion dies hard,'
his kiss says. 'Life is long.
I still can feel
and you are beautiful.'

III

The scene shifts to morning and sunlight and splendour of flags,
Great banners now drooping, now flaring in wind from the sea,
The clangorous tongues of the bells that resound and resound,
The cool milky jade of the water that licks at the steps
And the arrogant blackness of gondolas, blackness of swans.

JOAN MURRAY SIMPSON

SO FEW SLEEP SOUNDLY

Who can sleep soundly, dying through the dark?
The tired, the young, the innocent, the wise?
Not the first hunter deep inside his cave,
No mother, guardian of specific cries.

The sailor's heartbeat times his cradle's rocking,
Cannon sing lullaby in a soldier's ear;
Their senses guard them : let the rhythm falter
Once, and they wake; their sleeping minds can hear.

The old sleep little and lightly, as if any
Deep sleep might be that longest and last
Waiting to hold them tight : the young and strong
Don't want to sleep, days are used up too fast

To go to bed—and who would sleep alone?
They want too much, or do not care at all,
They question guilt, argue all night, wrestling
Our incubus, which must not ever fall.

Older and burdened, quite tired out at bedtime,
Father lies down to sleep, and though it may
Come, through his dreams they now pursue him—
The money or the words he chased all day.

Flat out, from dawn to dusk a well-attended
Referee-ed ring where doctors and medicines fight
Disease, the sick are left to go on counting
Bouts alone, when nurse-night blues the light.

We long for night, for sleep; absence, to smooth
And mend the daylong ravelling which makes
Us old : yet even a tired and happy child
Wakes screaming, chased by crocodiles and snakes.

Falling asleep, we gradually move
Backwards in time till we are almost apes,
The oldest, simplest places in the brain
The last to yield, quickest to sense fear's shapes;

For it is fear that keeps us all awake
And fear of death lies deepest; sleeping to keep
Alive, life watches : few can trust, few find
Peace in our nightly winding sheet of sleep.

SHIRLEY BRIDGES

SILENT IS THE HOUSE

Silent is the House—all are laid asleep;
One, alone, looks out o'er the snow wreaths deep;
Watching every cloud, dreading every breeze
That whirls the wildering drifts and bends the groaning trees.

Cheerful is the hearth, soft the matted floor;
Not one shivering gust creeps through pane or door;
The little lamp burns straight, its rays shoot strong and far.
I trim it well to be the Wanderer's guiding star.

Frown my haughty sire; chide my angry dame,
Set your slaves to spy, threaten me with shame;
But neither sire nor dame nor prying serf shall know
What angel nightly tracks that waste of winter snow.

What I love shall come like visitant of air,
Safe in secret power from lurking human snare;
Who loves me, no word of mine shall e'er betray,
Though for faith unstained my life must forfeit pay.

134

Burn then, little lamp; glimmer straight and clear—
Hush ! a rustling wing stirs, methinks, the air :
He for whom I wait, thus ever comes to me;
Strange Power ! I trust thy might; trust thou my constancy.

EMILY BRONTE
(1818–1848)

MASK AND ESSENCE

    Beneath the deep blue nightshade of the sky
    Dark bushes rise towards the dark cloud;
    Feet feel the ruts in the obscure road
    And lead the way. Sole
    Gleam upon the grassy verge
    The strange, low placed luminences,
    At friendly intervals.
    Reverently kneel, feel, take in palm
    A beetle,
    Small, pathetic wick
    Of the mystic light.

    In a barn,
    Where all was warm,
    A child
    Studied the candle
    Which made the shadows dance;
    Studied the blue cone
    Within the candle,
    Pushed the flame with its breath,
    To find the source,
    And found only the black stick,
    The wick.

    Kill not your candle.
    Revere your glow-worm.

JEAN OVERTON FULLER

135

THE WHITE HORSE

The white horse of death came steadily
From the heavy-dark woods
And over the bridge,
Shutting out with metallic clang,
For so many minutes,
The soft gurgling of the stream,
Which had drugged my drowsing spirit
With the serenity of limpid music.

Hypnotic the sound of hoof on stone
Drawing me, unwilling, to the window
Just a moment late,
So, when I gazed through the small, square pane,
Into a shimmering haze of moonlight,
The horse's form was already vanishing,
Unreal, floating almost into the cold,
Colourless space that was the night.

With the last clopped sound fading
In my ears, I turned back laughing
From the moon's strange magic
To the warm welcome of my bridal bed . . .

Not recognising, in that double ecstasy,
That death will call—and be forgotten—
While love compels anew a pulsing life.

RITA SPURR

THE QUESTION

On winter nights when the wind was cold,
And cried in the chimney, old, old,
And raged through the darkness and dashed on the stone
Of that ancient house where you sat alone,

With the tall arched windows North and West;
The lamp was calm and silver bright,
Like the full moon of a summer night,
And the fire was a rippling sheaf of light;
And the big black cat on the four-legged stool,
Round and sleek and beautiful,
Dozed with his paws curled under his breast.

O you alone, in the night awake,
The tempests clamour and shout and shake—
Is the lamp still steadfast, the fire still warm?
Bright and calm at the head of the stair,
Is there still a place like a lantern there,
A harbour lantern hung in the storm?

SYLVIA LYND
(1888–1952)

IT IS NOT LIKELY NOW

It is not likely now.
God's lion crouches low in jeopardy;
It is not likely that a step should sound
So late. Blame all on memory,
The tireless trickster who knows every path,
The way of every latch, mimics a pose in a chair
Truly to life, that the sad stranger Death
Stands back awkward, and unfamiliar.

It is less likely now.
A great fleet jewels the sky tonight,
Ships silver-lamped, and green, yellow,
And ruby; and the whole vast sea of midnight
Theirs. Who that could ride with that fleet would return
Here? I would not. I would ride and ride forever,
My deep light brilliant on the dark ocean,
A sign for my harmless and forgotten lover.

It will soon be dawn now,
For the little wolf-wind whimpers like a child.
Why should I wait and wait who have never found,
Never, anything by waiting? And have won the right
To that flawless freedom which is death-in-life : freedom
Never to be welcomed nor to welcome; never to turn the head
And wave; nor for the mind to hare leaping home
In advance. The only treasure of the living dead.

Nothing is likely now.
An angel has flung back the futile stone
And lion-Christ, God's darling, proud
And triumphing, strides freshly forth, done
Perhaps with death forever. Day without end?
Night is the flower of day; and at evening they come home
Who are coming, count them on the thumb of one hand.
Before you have finished, again evening will have come.

FRANCES BELLERBY

THE LIGHTHOUSE AT ACRE

(4 *a.m., April 6th,* 1962)

All night we sang, the invisible sea
Churning below, the deck-planks hard as flint
Yet cradling us with love, and scarlet lamps
Pricking the sky like poppies. We were cold,
Just five of us awake, and all the rest
Wise in their bunks and dreaming of the dawn,
And silence lapping us, and overhead
The massive darkness of two thousand years.

Why do we wait here, huddled in our rugs,
Clapping cold hands and bravely singing as
The clock-hands move to morning? Should we call

138

It hope of some unique experience,
Bravado and high spirits (we are young),
Or could it be religion after all?

"The wilderness shall blossom as the rose", we sang,
And "Ilka Moor Ba'at At", and "Clementine",
And still the night wore on, and still no dawn.

And then, at four o'clock, it must have been—
With sea and sky still black as all the years
Since Babylon, a needle-point of light
Sprang to the sky and vanished. Nothing more.
Cupping our dazzled eyes, pressed to the rails,
Straining against the darkness, silent now,
We watched for it again, our aching joints
Forgotten, and our very breathing stilled.

It was the Acre lighthouse, thrusting out
Its puny beam across the Stygian sea . . .
A shrouded lighthouse on a hidden shore.

And so, at last, we see the Promised Land.
Here is the first of it. In this faint spark,
This evanescent comet, is the reason
For staying and enduring, for the prayers
Of two millenia, for Warsaw, York,
The hope that did not die in Buchenwald,
For rebels, psalms and dreams . . . We thank Thee, God,
Who kept us five unworthy ones in life
(Sheltered and loved, knowing no suffering)
And nurtured us, and brought us to this season.

Within another hour the incredible dawn
Would come with golden flutes and tambourines
And blazing banners and triumphant song
To greet our ship; the harbour would fling wide
Its warm, white arms in welcome, trumpets sound
From Carmel, and the alabaster hills
Would clap their hands. Within a little while

The others would appear (the hidden ones,
Wise in their bunks and dreaming of that hour)
To throng the glowing deck, and strain across
The gilded rails, and laugh and weep, perhaps,
To see the long-awaited shore.
                              But now
For one brief moment, all the Universe
And all of Time were shrunken and compressed
Into a fitful needle-point of light
Half-glimpsed in darkness.
                         And I truly think
That if we five should live a hundred years
And see this land a hundred times again,
We should remember this above the rest—
The unseen Acre lighthouse tossing out
Into that sombre hour before the dawn
A spark to guide the wandering vessel home.

PAMELA   MELNIKOFF

ANGER'S FREEING POWER

I had a dream three walls stood up wherein a raven bird
Against the walls did beat himself and was not that absurd?

For sun and rain beat in that cell that had its fourth wall free
And daily blew the summer shower and the rain came
    presently.

And all the pretty summertime and all the winter too
That foolish bird did beat himself till he was black and blue.

Rouse up, rouse up, my raven bird, fly by the open wall
You make a prison of a place that is not one at all.

I took my raven by the hand, Oh come, I said, my Raven,
And I will take you by the hand and you shall fly to heaven.

And oh he sobbed and oh he sighed and in a fit he lay
Until two fellow ravens came and stood outside to say :

You wretched bird, conceited lump
You well deserve to pine and thump.

See now a wonder, mark it well
My bird rears up in angry spell,

Oh do I then ? he says, and careless flies
O'er flattened wall at once to heaven's skies.

And in my dream I watched him go
And I was glad, I loved him so,

Yet when I woke my eyes were wet
To think Love had not freed my pet.

Anger it was that won him hence
As only Anger taught him sense.

Often my tears fall in a shower
Because of Anger's freeing power.

STEVIE SMITH

'HOPE IS THE THING WITH FEATHERS'

Hope is the thing with feathers
That perches in the soul,
And sings the tune without the words,
And never stops at all,

And sweetest in the gale is heard;
And sore must be the storm
That could abash the little bird
That kept so many warm.

141

I've heard it in the chillest land,
And on the strangest sea;
Yet never, in extremity,
It asked a crumb of me.

EMILY DICKINSON*
(U.S.A.)
(1850–1886)

from THE FLOWERING OF THE ROD (V)

Satisfied, unsatisfied,
satiated or numb with hunger,

this is the eternal urge,
this is the despair, the desire to equilibriate

the eternal variant;
you understand that insistent calling,

that demand of a given moment,
the will to enjoy, the will to live,

not merely the will to endure,
the will to flight, the will to achievement,

the will to rest after long flight;
but who knows the desperate urge

of those others—actual or perhaps now
mythical birds—who see but find no rest

till they drop from the highest point of the spiral
or fall from the innermost centre of the ever-narrowing circle?

for they remember, they remember, as they sway and hover,
what once was—they remember, they remember—

they will not swerve—they have known bliss,
the fruit that satisfies—they have come back—

what if the islands are lost? what if the waters
cover the Hesperides? they would rather remember—

remember the golden apple-trees;
O, do not pity them, as you watch them drop one by one,

for they fall exhausted, numb, blind
but in certain ecstasy

for theirs is the hunger
for Paradise.

H.D. (HILDA DOOLITTLE)
(U.S.A.)
(1886–1961)

MOUNTAIN FLORA

As the plant on the smooth of the hill
That sees not the deep and the height,
That knows not the might
Of the whole—
I am rooted and grounded in him,
The small leaves of my soul
Thrust up from his will.

I know not the terrible peak,
The white and ineffable Thought,
Whence the hill-torrents flow
And my nurture is brought.
I am little and meek;
I dare not to lift
My look to his snow,
But drink, drop by drop, of its gift.

Some say, on the face
Of that ultimate height
Small plants have their place :
Rapt far from our sight
In the solitude strange
Where the infinite Dream mounts range beyond range
To the infinite Sky, there they grow.

Where the intellect faints
In the silence and cold,
There, humble and glad, their petals unfold.
As the innocent bell
Of the Least Soldanella thrusts up through the snow,
So the hearts of the saints
On the terrible height of the Godhead may dwell;
Held safe by the Will
As we, on the smooth of the hill.

EVELYN UNDERHILL
(1875–1941)

ON PLANTING A TREE

For pride of life
I plant this tree.
Age that gives it strength
shall wither me.
Remember me living. I
need nothing when I die.

In death I shall
not be alone :
all my loved ghosts shall bury me home.
All my sad hopes shall there
grow green and feed the air.

Laughter shall rise
in my tree
when the roots
take hold of me.
When flesh and bone are dead
I shall be leaf instead.

KAREN GERSHON

WHAT ARE YEARS?

What is our innocence,
what is our guilt? All are
    naked, none is safe. And whence
is courage : the unanswered question,
the resolute doubt,—
dumbly calling, deafly listening—that
in misfortune, even death,
    encourages others
    and in its defeat, stirs

the soul to be strong? He
sees deep and is glad, who
    accedes to mortality
and in his imprisonment, rises
upon himself as
the sea in a chasm, struggling to be
free and unable to be,
    in its surrendering
    finds its continuing.

So he who strongly feels
behaves. The very bird,
    grown taller as he sings, steels
his form straight up. Though he is captive,
his mighty singing

145

says, satisfaction is a lowly
thing, how pure a thing is joy.
    This is mortality,
    this is eternity.

MARIANNE MOORE
(U.S.A.)

HYMN TO EARTH

Farewell, incomparable element,
Whence man arose, where he shall not return;
And hail, imperfect urn
Of his last ashes, and his firstborn fruit;
Farewell, the long pursuit,
And all the adventures of his discontent;
The voyages which sent
His heart averse from home :
Metal of clay, permit him that he come
To thy slow-burning fire as to a hearth;
Accept him as a particle of earth.

Fire, being divided from the other three,
It lives removed, or secret at the core;
Most subtle of the four,
When air flies not, nor water flows,
It disembodied goes,
Being light, elixir of the first decree,
More volatile than he;
With strength and power to pass
Through space, where never his least atom was :
He has no part in it, save as his eyes
Have drawn its emanation from the skies.
A wingless creature heavier than air,
He is rejected of its quintessence;
Coming and going hence,

146

In the twin minutes of his birth and death,
He may inhale as breath,
As breath relinquish heaven's atmosphere,
Yet in it have no share,
Nor can survive therein
Where its outer edge is filtered pure and thin :
It doth but lend its crystal to his lungs
For his early crying, and his final songs.

The element of water has denied
Its child; it is no more his element;
It never will relent;
Its silver harvests are more sparsely given
Than the rewards of heaven,
And he shall drink cold comfort at its side :
The water is too wide :
The seamew and the gull
Feather a nest made soft and pitiful
Upon its foam; he has not any part
In the long swell of sorrow at its heart.

Hail and farewell, belovèd element,
Whence he departed, and his parent once;
See where thy spirit runs
Which for so long hath had the moon to wife;
Shall this support his life
Until the arches of the waves be bent
And grow shallow and spent?
Wisely it cast him forth
With his dead weight of burden nothing worth
Leaving him, for the universal years,
A little sea-water to make his tears.

Hail, element of earth, receive thy own,
And cherish, at thy charitable breast,
This man, this mongrel beast :
He ploughs the sand, and, at his hardest need,
He sows himself for seed;

147

He ploughs the furrow, and in this lies down
Before the corn is grown;
Between the apple bloom
And the ripe apple is sufficient room
In time, and matter, to consume his love
And make him parcel of a cypress grove.

Receive him as thy lover for an hour
Who will not weary, by a longer stay,
The kind embrace of clay;
Even within thine arms he is dispersed
To nothing, as at first;
The air flings downward from its four-quartered tower
Him whom the flames devour;
At the full tide, at the flood,
The sea is mingled with his salty blood :
The traveller dust, although the dust be vile
Sleeps as thy lover for a little while.

ELINOR WYLIE
(U.S.A.)
(1885–1928)

RANDOM HARVEST

HINTERLAND

I like the backs of houses. Fronts are smug,
Stiff and formal, masks which smile at neighbours.
These roofs, shrugging, relaxed, these sun-warmed bricks,
Smooth, rounded bays, they are like lovers in bed
At ease, knowing and known. Cats stalk here.
The wagging lines of washing wave, the knops
Of hollyhocks knock and stroke the walls. A sunflower
Rises, bearded god with a black face.
And the swarthy, smiling, grape-bloomed neighbours stand
Amazed between the vines, the flowers, the walls,
Themselves placid yet savage deities
Of these long gardens, of these hinterlands,
Green, warm and secret territory, here
Like love behind the streets' correct façade.
Love, fierce and unexpected, sharp, uneven,
Sun and flower, the darkness and the sap
Surging through leaf and body, the quick flashed
Recognition of opened windows, white
Glances meeting, and doors, doors open wide.

MARGARET STANLEY-WRENCH

MEETING-HOUSE HILL

I must be mad, or very tired,
When the curve of a blue bay beyond a railroad track
Is shrill and sweet to me like the sudden springing of a tune,
And the sight of a white church above thin trees in a city
    square
Amazes my eyes as though it were the Parthenon.
Clear, reticent, superbly final,
With the pillars of its portico refined to a cautious elegance,
It dominates the weak trees,
And the shot of its spire

151

Is cool, and candid,
Rising into an unresisting sky.
Strange meeting-house

Pausing a moment upon a squalid hill-top.
I watch the spire sweeping the sky,
I am dizzy with the movement of the sky,
I might be watching a mast
With its royals set full
Straining before a two-reef breeze.
I might be sighting a tea-clipper,
Tacking into the blue bay,
Just back from Canton
With her hold full of green and blue porcelain,
And a Chinese coolie leaning over the rail
Gazing at the white spire
With dull sea-spent eyes.

AMY LOWELL*
(U.S.A.)

THE ROMANCE OF THE SWAN'S NEST

"So the dreams depart,
So the fading phantoms flee
And the sharp reality
Now must act its part."
WESTWOOD'S "Beads from a Rosary"

Little Ellie sits alone,
'Mid the beeches of a meadow,
By a stream-side on the grass,
And the trees are showering down
Doubles of their leaves in shadow
On her shining hair and face.

152

She has thrown her bonnet by,
  And her feet she has been dipping
    In the shallow water's flow :
Now she holds them nakedly
  In her hands all sleek and dripping
    While she rocketh to and fro.

Little Ellie sits alone
  And the smile she softly uses
    Fills the silence like a speech,
While she thinks what shall be done
  And the sweetest pleasure chooses
    For her future within reach.

Little Ellie in her smile
  Chooses—"I will have a lover
    Riding on a steed of steeds :
He shall love me without guile,
  And to *him* I will discover
    The swan's nest among the reeds.

"And the steed shall be red-roan,
  And the lover shall be noble,
    With an eye that takes the breath :
And the lute he plays upon
  shall strike ladies into trouble
    As his sword strikes men to death.

"And the steed it shall be shod
  All in silver, housed in azure
    And the mane shall swim the wind;
And the hoofs along the sod
  Shall flash onward and keep measure
    Till the shepherds look behind.

"But my lover will not prize
  All the glory that he rides in,
    When he gazes in my face :

He will say, 'O love, thine eyes
　　Build the shrine my soul abides in,
　　　　And I kneel here for thy grace!'

"Then, ay, then he shall kneel low,
　　With the red-roan steed anear him
　　　　Which shall seem to understand,
Till I answer, 'Rise and go!
　　For the world must love and fear him
　　　　Whom I gift with heart and hand.'

"Then he will arise so pale,
　　I shall feel my own lips tremble
　　　　With a *yes* I must not say,
Nathless, maiden-brave, 'Farewell,'
　　I will utter, and dissemble—
　　　　'Light tomorrow with today!'

Then he'll ride among the hills
　　To the wide world past the river,
　　　　There to put away all wrong;
To make straight distorted wills;
　　And to empty the broad quiver
　　　　Which the wicked bear along.

"Three times shall a young foot-page
　　Swim the stream and climb the mountain
　　　　And kneel down beside my feet—
'Lo, my master sends this gage,
　　Lady, for thy pity's counting!
　　　　What wilt thou exchange for it?'

"And the first time I will send
　　A white rosebud for a guerdon,
　　　　And the second time a glove;
But the third time—I may bend
　　From my pride, and answer—'Pardon
　　　　If he comes to take my love.'

"Then the young foot-page will run,
　　Then my lover will ride faster,
　　　Till he kneeleth at my knee :
'I am a duke's eldest son,
　　Thousand serfs do call me master,
　　　But, O Love. I love but *thee* !'

"He will kiss me on the mouth
　　Then, and lead me as a lover
　　　Through the crowds that praise his deeds;
And, when soul-tied by one troth,
　　Unto *him* I will discover
　　　The swan's nest among the reeds."

Little Ellie, with her smile
　　Not yet ended, rose up gaily,
　　　Tied the bonnet, donned the shoe,
And went homeward, round a mile,
　　Just to see, as she did daily
　　　What more eggs were with the two.

Pushing through the elm-tree copse,
　　Winding up the stream light-hearted,
　　　Where the osier pathway leads,
Past the boughs she stoops—and stops.
　　Lo, the wild swan had deserted,
　　　And a rat had gnawed the reeds !

Ellie went home sad and slow.
　　If she found the lover ever
　　　With his red-roan steed of steeds,
Sooth I know not; but I know
　　She could never show him—never
　　　That swan's nest among the reeds !

ELIZABETH BARRETT BROWNING
(1806–1861)

THE WINDOW

(For Stephen)

The mauve light of evening fills the room
    Like a crushed scabious;
And you, at the window, watch through it, in your head
Those thoughts that I may never know you think,
    Nor wish to know,
Because a country, then, would be robbed of its mystery,
Where twilights fall rarer for being guessed at.
    I know what you see :
Pink may on the single tree; slated
Shed; the garden falling away to buttercups;
    Weeds beyond,
And outside these the sea we both are drunk with,
    Watered like silk,
Or a Japanese print, you said, painted with gulls
    And corks on the water.
The sand is covered, and nothing of the children remains
But a sun-bonnet floating beside a castle, down,
    And a spade on the steps;
While the top stones wait till the wave, that is hardly there,
    Shall make them sea.
'Look at that star !' you continue, 'The brightest star I've ever
    seen,
'Except Venus, once in January, over the Atlantic,
    'Shaming the moon.
'If you watch a star, you can almost see it climbing,
'Can't you ? Now the cuckoo's joining tune
    'With sparrow and thrush :
'What sillies they are those others : thousands of years
'She's gone on laying her eggs in their nests, and they
    'Have never noticed !'
Your cigarette sparks up; and the nightingale,
That is almost too much poetry, hustles the night.
    'Look ! Ah, listen !
Come over here !' you say, though your lips are silent;
    But I will not obey,

Because this moment is one of my mind's own seeing,
   And with me for ever;
You looking out of the window, part of so much,
   Unconscious of my loving.

ODE TO APHRODITE

Rainbow-robed, immortal Aphrodite
Wile-weaving daughter of Zeus,
I implore you,
Do not with moan and grief
Lady, break my soul;

But come hither—
If ever it be said
That you have heard
My cry from afar
Have ever left
Your father's golden home
Coming in your yoked chariot
Guided by the dear, swift sparrows
Who, whirling their wise wings
Through the skies
Above the dark-wombed Earth,
Beat their feathered way
Through the middle air.

Moreover, O Blessed One,
It was with a smile
On your pure, undying face
That you asked :
'What ails you, wheedling one,
What new misfortune, my prattling bird,

Tell me what now, above all,
Your frantic heart desires.
Whose surrender do you yearn for—
Who, Sappho, opposes you?

For, whoso would escape you,
Will quickly pursue—
Whoso disdains your gifts
Will accept.
And whoso loves you not
Speedily will love,
Whatsoever the struggle'.

Come then now to me!
Release me from the weight
Of my suffering.
Accomplish all that my soul
Longs for—
Grant me my desire—
Be Thou, Thyself, my Comrade-in-Arms.

SAPPHO OF LESBOS
(6th century B.C.)
(trans. ROSS MACAULAY)

WE SHALL COME NO MORE

So then we came to the Island,
Lissom and young, with the radiant sun in our faces;
Anchored in long quiet lines the ships were waiting,
Giants, asleep in the peace of the dark-blue harbour.
Ashore we leapt, to seek the magic adventure
Up the valley at noontide,
Where shimmering lay the fields of asphodel.

O Captain of our Voyage
What of the Dead?
Dead days, dead hopes, dead loves, dead dreams,
*   dead sorrows—*
O Captain of our Voyage
Do the dead walk again?

Today we look for the Island,
Older, a little tired, our confidence waning;
On the ocean bed the shattered ships lie crumbling
Where lost men's bones gleam white in the shrouded silence.
The Island waits but we shall never find it,
Nor see the dark-blue harbour
Where twilight falls on fields of asphodel.

VERA BRITTAIN

GOING NORTH FOR CHRISTMAS

Uncertain as rain the future lies submerged
Like the flat flooded fields that spread into the distance
On either side of the track, sad, grey witnesses
Of November storms, and like the bare trees that rise
From their own images, my grief is reflected in these waters.

Dark at four the illuminated station welcomes
The train and red and green signals direct it;
Glimpsing them behind as the train rounds a bend
They reassure; they have the power of absolute wisdom;
The trains trust them and come safely to their destinations.

For ships that traffic across the sea there is the lighthouse
And the foghorn; hearing its drear message when I reach
The end of my journey I know I have come back to a world
Where bedtime in winter meant falling asleep to this unending
    woe,
And I woke at half-past seven to the shipyard's buzzer.

159

I have come back to a town on the edge of the sea and life
Whose laws were as immutable as the urgent flash from the
    pier
And the lament of the estuary, but the sea was a way out;
Cold waves that lifted me in summer and crashed over sea
    walls
In winter set me free and I sailed in the riding ships.

Dangerous and deep as fantasy, I still need this sea,
Choosing to stay where I can see it from my window;
When I wake in the morning it is calm and glows as the sun
Flowers in the mist and drops a golden road
On its greyness from the fisherman's bay to the priory on the
    headland.

The lighthouse remains hidden and mist still blurs
The horizon, but as the sun rises, sea and sky
Grow blue, breakers sparkle, air and water
Are as calm as on a summer's day and I walk by the shore
As in childhood letting the spray splash my face.

Yet the child who was dolphin and captain has been swept
    away
By a more tempestuous sea than daydreams knew;
I have sailed this sea alone without quadrant, map
Or compass and when I set forth again from this harbour
Foghorn and lighthouse will guide me no farther than its
    mouth.

ROSEMARY JOSEPH

THE SURFER

He thrust his joy against the weight of the sea,
climbed through, slid under those long banks of foam—
(hawthorn hedges in spring, thorns in the face stinging).

How his brown strength drove through the hollow and coil
of green-through weirs of water!
Muscle of arm thrust down long muscle of water.
And swimming so, went out of sight
where mortal, masterful, frail, the gulls went wheeling
in air, as he in water, with delight.

Turn home, the sun goes down; swimmer, turn home
Last leaf of gold vanishes from the sea-curve.
Take the big roller's shoulder, speed and swerve.
Come to the long beach home like a gull diving.

For on the sand the grey-wolf sea lies snarling;
cold twilight wind splits the waves' hair and shows
the bones they worry in their wolf-teeth. O, wind blows,
and sea crouches on sand, fawning and mouthing;
drops there and snatches again, drops and again snatches
its broken toys, its whitened pebbles and shells.

JUDITH WRIGHT
(Australia)

THE SERPENT

Twisting her conscience in a coil of words
His subtle tongue brought silence on the birds
While promises fell drop by drop upon
Her ears like oil.
He breathed on bud-green thought, hour after hour,
Stroked petals of her being wide apart
Till fancy flared into a crimson flower.

Fiercer than drought he ravished her— ·
The sliding river shrank into its bed;
A cactus bristled from dry lips of mud—
And offered her a fruit, barbaric-red.

Biting into white flesh underneath
She melted in the pressure of his mind,
Drank his vine-cool, wine-inflaming words,
Blind to impartial judgment of the sun.

Darkly her fate was spun.
Plucking the rose, oblivious of the briar,
She languished on the penetrating spine,
Then coil by coil, mounting a spire of air,
Ecstasy crescendoed to the stars,
Sank voiceless in the rain.
Her fluttering soul, a heap of feathers, stirred
As a gate clanged in her brain.

PHOEBE HESKETH

PRESENT TENSE

Time : counted by hunting, killing
devouring, sleeping, and waking again
with stomach flaccid and hungering.
Pain : not measured by better or worse,
yesterday or to-morrow :
only by nowness and lintels of night.
Now : is what spares them from anticipation.
Pricked ears, alerted eyes, hair
ridged on backbone, adrenalin coursing,
is sudden and now.

Living is now, not was not going to be.
Fright and flight, call for a mate,
squeeze of womb, cry of new-born,
dark hole of dying, happens simultaneously.
To-day they catch their first prey,
to-day they limp in autumnal forests,
for their lives are always in the present tense.

162

Yet memory prows in the border of their brains,
though the first ape that walked erect
forgot his yesterdays.

ARMITAGE HARGREAVES
(Canada)

PRIZE-FIGHTER

Conditioned by two split things—
Atoms and seconds—
He felt both
In the bright explosion
Between fog and night
As the fist hit him.

Moments before he had been
Tiger shut
In too small a cage.
Sure-footed he'd followed
The teasing shadow
That danced and evaded.

Then dancer became gorilla.
Fog fell.
His arms played puppet
To his sliding brain,
And his nerves thinned
To spider-threads.

And then it hit him—
A seventh wave
Smacking a cliff.
Pieces of him
Broke off. All crashed
On the back-sucking pebbles.

163

He did not feel the vibrating
Ground, nor the wind
Made by the shouting.
The darkness, the rest
Ached for, he had;
But he never knew.

MARGERY SMITH

THE DIAMOND CUTTER

Not what the light will do but how he shapes it
And what particular colours it will bear,

And something of the climber's concentration
Seeing the white peak, setting the right foot there.

Not how the sun was plausible at morning
Nor how it was distributed at noon,

And not how much the single stone could show
But rather how much brilliance it would shun;

Simply a paring down, a cleaving to
One object, as the star-gazer who sees

One single comet polished by its fall
Rather than countless, untouched galaxies.

ELIZABETH JENNINGS

THE MIRROR

Jan Vermeer Speaks

Time that is always gone stays still
A moment in this quiet room.
Nothing exists but what we know,
The mirror gathers in the world,
Time and the world. And I shall hold
All summers in a stroke of gold.

Twilight, and one last fall of sun
That slants across the window-sill,
And, mirrored darkly in the glass
(Can paint attempt that unlit void?)
All night, oblivion, is stayed
Within the curtain's folded shade.

Upon the table bread and wine.
The earthen pitcher's perfect curve
Once spun upon the potter's wheel
Is pivot of the turning world,
Still centre where my peace abides,
Round moon that draws all restless tides.

There, it is done. The vision fades
And Time moves on. Oh you who praise
This tangled, broken web of paint,
I paint reflections in a glass :
Who look on Truth with mortal sight
Are blinded in its blaze of light.

ROSEMARY DOBSON
(Australia)

THE LAST ENEMY

(after 'The Siege of Constantinople' by Delacroix)

The conquerors are sad whose victory so often
is Phyrrhic : climbing again to their chosen height
they lean on leaning mounts in a vague desperation
whom neither massacre nor rape delight.

Was it for this they left the throne and the homestead
wearing too heavy helmets Viking nor Plantagenet
would acknowledge, cluttered with inherited armour,
cloaks, plumes and pennon : drooping rein, slack bit?

The horse is wisest : he knows death when he sees it,
snuffs the blood-reek with terror in his eye
unable to contend with that reality
not conveyed by the touch on the rein, the pressed goad
(willing to die for his god, but he must be spurred to die).

And these have lost the spur : the landscape's indifference,
the fading Grail, the beckoning mirage, Faith,
elude them still who have laid siege to Death.

ELISABETH CLUER

IMAGES

Again this morning trembles on the swift stream the image of
    the sun
Dimmed and pulsing shadow insubstantial of the bright one
That scatters innumerable as eyes these discs of light scaling
    the water.
From a dream foolish and sorrowful I return to this day's
    morning.
And words are said as the thread slips away of a ravelled story :
'The new-born have forgotten that great burden of pain
World has endured before you came.'

A marble Eros sleeps in peace unbroken by the fountain
Out of what toils of ever-suffering love conceived?
Only the gods can bear our memories:
We in their lineaments serene
That look down on us with untroubled gaze
Fathom our own mind and what it is
Cleansed from the blood we shed, the deaths we die.

How many tears have traced those still unfading presences
Who on dim walls depict spirit's immortal joy?
They look from beyond time on sorrow upon sorrow of ours
And of our broken many our whole truth one angel tells,
Ingathers to its golden abiding form the light we scatter,
And winged with unconsuming fire our shattered image
reassembles.
My load of memory is almost full;
But here and now I see once more mirrored the semblance of
the radiant source
Whose image the fleet waters break but cannot bear away.

KATHLEEN RAINE

THE CHARIOT

(*Giacometti*)

She is cut away : a rising
spider woman from stopped wheels.

Tearing the skin from cogs and spokes
the thighs grow from the block
to something like a goddess.

When no one looks she makes
reins from the air,
strength steals from the long vacuum
her speed displaced.

167

Stencil rider draws her arc—
fleshless levels fat Olympus,
and out of its fire strut the wings
and flown circles of her weightless car
immortal in the studded curve
of incipient sexless career.

ANGELA LANGFIELD*

THE BRONZE OF POSEIDON

I

The bronze head came from the sea,
And the eyes were smooth from long years
Of the deep green underwaters.
Only the head, bold with bull-curls,
Left from the long, anonymous
Wrack of the centuries. Yet
The bold of that head, and the swell
Of muscle and tendon, the pull
Of strength and of vigour told
Of the god-form, dreamed, conceived,
Bronze-framed, destroyed, unclothed
Into dust by the years. In its pride
The bronze head lay, shard of a god,
That sang, like a dream of wine
New-pressed when the sea was young.

II

The bronzed man came from the sea,
And his eyes were strong from long years
Of scanning the deep green waters.
Only the head, bold with bull-curls,
Rose from the square, anonymous
Set of the collar. Yet

The bold of that head, and the swell
Of muscle and tendon, the pull
Of strength and of vigour told
Of the god-form held, concealed,
Defamed, destroyed by clothes
And the cramping of years. In his pride
The bronzed man stood there—a god
Who sang his dreams (born of wine)
Of years when his love was young.

III

The scholar came in from the street,
And his eyes were bleared from long years
Of pondering deep his quartos.
He peered at "a head, bold with bull-curls",
And left, planning long and ponderous
Tomes on the art-form. Yet
The sailor's head, bold with the swell
Of muscle and tendon, the pull
Of strength and of vigour told
Him nothing. A god is conceived
Bronze-framed, pure, classic, unclothed . . .
Art keeps, through all years, its pride!
But the bronzed man lurched, like a god
Flushed with a dreaming of wine
New-pressed before art was young.

VERA RICH

GREEK STATUES

These I have never touched but only looked at.
If you could say that stillness meant surrender
These are surrendered.
Yet their large audacious gestures signify surely

169

Remonstrance, reprisal? What have they left to lose
But the crumbling away by rain or time? Defiance
For them is a dignity, a declaration.

Odd how one wants to touch not simply stare,
To run one's fingers over the flanks and arms,
Not to possess, rather to be possessed.
Bronze is bright to the eye but under the hands
Is cool and calming. Gods into silent metal :

To stone also, not to the palpable flesh.
Incarnations are elsewhere and more human,
Something concerning us; but these are other.
It is as if something infinite, remote
Permitted intrusion. It is as if these blind eyes
Exposed a landscape precious with grapes and olives :
And our probing hands move not to grasp but praise.

ELIZABETH JENNINGS

STATUES

They more than we are what we are,
Serenity and joy
We lost or never found,
The forms of heart's desire,
We gave them what we could not keep,
We made them what we cannot be.

Their kingdom is our dream, but who can say
If they or we
Are dream or dreamer, signet or clay;
If the most perfect be most true
These faces pure, these bodies poised in thought
Are substance of our form,
And we the confused shadows cast.

Growing towards their prime, they take our years away,
And from our deaths they rise
Immortal in the life we lose.
The gods consume us, but restore
More than we were :
We love that they may be,
They are, that we may know.

KATHLEEN RAINE

FIRST AND LAST THINGS

ANNUNCIATION

The quick pale fingers of Sister Tutor
Springing from bare wrists, the cuffs rolled back,
Deftly unscrew the squat womb's lid.

We cannot identify its contents
Amorphous in the dull formalin-fuddled
Liquid; but her quick bright voice

Steadies the creeping sickness. Finger-tips
Delve. "Come along, little fella."
She lifts him out, the five months foetus,

Whose putty-coloured indiarubber limbs,
Thin as bird-bones, curl coldly
On a forgotten pillow of warm flesh.

The watching eyes of the green girls
Are still as pools. Only a long
Long exhalation of pure pity,

Strangely unanimous, flickers and dies
Momentarily over the packed membranes
Of unexpanded lungs. We breathe for him.

"Look, even the little tongue is perfect."
Pinching the wrinkled cheeks so that the mouth opens.
It does not squeak "Mama". This one is real,

From whose shrunken abdomen still snakes
Thick and tortuous, the cord that carried life
Generously at first, but death in the end.

The quick starched fingers of Sister Tutor
Force him again through the jar's mouth. Formalin stings
The eyes; he floats in a sac of primal tears.

175

Out file the green girls into careless streets.
The public gardens, prim with flowers, invite
No sudden revelations; yet limbs stiffen

Against strange delicate fibrillations
That will not be denied; within each one,
Immaculately conceived, a new life stirs.

MONICA DITMAS*

WOMAN'S SONG

O move in me, my darling,
for now the sun must rise;
the sun that will draw open
the lids upon your eyes.

O wake in me, my darling.
The knife of day is bright
to cut the thread that binds you
within the flesh of night.

Today I lose and find you
whom yet my blood would keep—
would weave and sing around you
the spells and songs of sleep.

None but I shall know you
as none but I have known;
yet there's a death and a maiden
who wait for you alone;

So move in me, my darling,
whose debt I cannot pay.
Pain and the dark must claim you,
and passion and the day.

JUDITH WRIGHT
(Australia)

Down the porphyry stair
Headlong into the air
The boy has come : he crouches there
A tender startled creature
With a fawn's ears and hair-spring poise
Alert to every danger
Aghast at every noise.
A blue blink
From under squeezed-up lids
As mauve as iris buds
Is gone as quickly as a bird's bright wink.
Gone—but as if his soul had looked an instant through the
    chink.
And perfect as his shell-like nails,
Close as are to the flower its petals,
My love unfolded with him.
Yet till this moment what was he to me?
Conjecture and analogy;
Conceived and yet unknown;
Behind this narrow barrier of bone
Distant as any foreign land could be.

> *I have seen the light of day*
> *Was it sight or taste or smell?*
> *Where have I been, who can tell?*
> *What I shall be, who can say?*

He floats in life as a lily in the pool
Free and yet rooted;
And strong though seeming frail,
Like the ghost fritillary
That trails its first-appearing bud
As though too weak to raise it from the mud,
But is stronger than you dream,
And soon will lift its paper lantern
High upon an arched and sinewy stem.

His smiles are all largesse,
Need ask for no return,
Since give and take are meaningless
To one who gives by needing
And takes our love for granted
And grants a favour even by his greed.
The ballet of his twirling hands
His chirping and his loving sounds,
Perpetual expectation
Perpetual surprise—
Not a lifetime satisfies
For watching, every thing he does
We wish him to do always.

> Only in a lover's eyes
> Shall I be so approved again;
> Only the other side of pain
> Can truth again be all I speak,
> Or I again possess
> A saint's hilarious carelessness.

ANNE RIDLER

STILLBIRTH

Labour was normal, a birth, like any other.
But long, for bearing nothing but a stone;
Pushing a stone of pain uphill for hours
Gasping for breath.
Hope did not die till later.
I had been heavy, a stagnant pool, no stir
No beat of heart, hands. Then
This cataclysm that seemed to presage life.
But, at the end, no cry.

Under the half-death of the chloroform
I heard the nurse laugh, joking with the doctor,

Thinking I could not hear. I knew, then
And a weak rage rose in my throat
That it was mine they looked at and held light.
I would have snatched it from them
carried it in my mouth to my lair
With animal groans, and licked it back to life.

They took it from me, told me, all's for the best
And shut it in a box. What else to do
With something, not quite rubbish?
They did it decently,
Washed the cold face with colder drops of pity,
Baptised it for luck,
And put it in the earth where it belonged.

I never saw the features I had made,
The hands I had felt groping
For the life I tried to give, and could not.
But still, I sometimes dream I hear it crying
Lost somewhere and unfed,
Shut in a cupboard, or lying in the snow,
And I search the night, and call, as though to rescue
Part of myself, from the grave of things undone.

BARBARA NOEL SCOTT

UNKNOWN GIRL IN THE MATERNITY WARD

Child, the current of your breath is six days long.
You lie, a small knuckle on my white bed;
lie, fisted like a snail, so small and strong
at my breast. Your lips are animals; you are fed
with love. At first hunger is not wrong.
The nurses nod their caps; you are shepherded
down starch halls with the other unnested throng
in wheeling baskets. You tip like a cup; your head
moving to my touch. You sense the way we belong.

179

But this is an institution bed.
You will not know me very long.

The doctors are enamel. They want to know
the facts. They guess about the man who left me,
some pendulum soul, going the way men go
and leave you full of child. But our case history
stays blank. All I did was let you grow.
Now we are here for all the ward to see.
They thought I was strange, although
I never spoke a word. I burst empty
of you, letting you learn how the air is so.
The doctors chart the riddle they ask of me
and I turn my head away. I do not know.

Yours is the only face I recognise.
Bone at my bone, you drink my answers in.
Six times a day I prize
your need, the animals of your lips, your skin
growing warm and plump. I see your eyes
lifting their tents. They are blue stones, they begin
to outgrow their moss. You blink in surprise
and I wonder what you can see, my funny kin,
as you trouble my silence. I am a shelter of lies.
Should I learn to speak again, or hopeless in
such sanity will I touch some face I recognise?

Down the hall the baskets start back. My arms
fit you like a sleeve, they hold
catkins of your willows, the wild bee farms
of your nerves, each muscle and fold
of your first days. Your old man's face disarms
the nurses. But the doctors return to scold
me. I speak. It is you my silence harms.
I should have known; I should have told
them something to write down. My voice alarms
my throat. 'Name of father—none.' I hold
you and name you bastard in my arms.
And now that's that. There is nothing more
that I can say or lose.

Others have traded life before
and could not speak. I tighten to refuse
your owling eyes, my fragile visitor.
I touch your cheeks, like flowers. You bruise
against me. We unlearn. I am a shore
rocking you off. You break from me. I choose
your only way, my small inheritor
and hand you off, trembling the selves we lose.
Go child, who is my sin and nothing more.

ANNE SEXTON
(U.S.A.)

THE GAZE

Your light is not yet broken :
Single the seven colours stream
In one white eyebeam from your self to mine.
My look, refracted and coloured by desires
Brings home a half-truth, but when you look at me
It is as though you had thrown a line
Out from your cradle to draw my image back.
Mirrors return the image which we show them,
But like a thinker, when you reflect on me
You take me in. And this without deceit,
Since you are open and looks are free.

God is the source on which you should gaze like that.
I am not worth it; looking at me you must learn
Selection, and suppress some part of the truth,
For art or kindness' sake. But not for love's.
For love (which has no need to blame or praise)
Wakens that white beam again, reminding me
That I was born for this, to watch my Maker
Ever, with such a humble, thirsty gaze.

ANNE RIDLER

THE BAIRN

Babe, by your helplessness
Conjure pity in my breast :
By your little wailing cry
Bring forth all my bravery.

Wake, by your perfect trust
Love that had turned to dust :
In your sleeping, little lad,
Give me back the faith I had.

Bring me back humility
As I sense your purity;
Feel the intake of your breath
Driving forth my fear of death.

Babe, who re-created me,
Preserve me this felicity.

ROSAMUND GREENWOOD

CHILD WAKING

The child sleeps in the daytime,
With his abandoned, with his jetsam look,
On the bare mattress, across the cot's corner;
Covers and toys thrown out, a routine labour.

Relaxed in sleep and light,
Face upwards, never so clear a prey to eyes;
Like a walled town surprised out of the air
—All his life called in, yet all laid bare

To the enemy above—
He has taken cover in daylight, gone to ground
In his own short length, his body strong in bleached
blue cotton and his arms outstretched.

Now he opens eyes but not
To see at first; they reflect the light like snow,
And I wait in doubt if he sleeps or wakes, till I see
Slight pain of effort at the boundary,

And hear how the trifling wound
Of bewilderment fetches a caverned cry
As he crosses out of sleep—at once to recover
his place and poise, and smile as I lift him over.

But I recall the blue-
White snowfield of his eyes empty of sight
High between dream and day, and think how there
The soul might rise visible as a flower.

E. J. SCOVELL

OLD WOMAN

So much she caused she cannot now account for
As she stands watching day return, the cool
Walls of the house moving towards the sun.
She puts some flowers in a vase and thinks
    'There is not much I can arrange
In here and now, but flowers are suppliant

As children never were. And love is now
A flicker of memory, my body is
My own entirely. When I lie at night

183

I gather nothing now into my arms,
    No child or man, and where I live
Is what remains when men and children go.'

Yet she owns more than residue of lives
That she has marked and altered. See how she
Warns time from too much touching her possessions
By keeping flowers fed by polishing
    Her fine old silver. Gratefully
She sees her own glance printed on grandchildren.

Drawing the curtains back and opening windows
Every morning now, she feels her years
Grow less and less. Time puts no burden on
Her now she does not need to measure it.
    It is acceptance she arranges,
And her own life she places in the vase.

ELIZABETH JENNINGS

THE DARK RIDER

The dark-plumed rider striking the iron door
a roaring rearing horse
and the storm drumming on the hard ground—
this was his anger.

And he was growing old.
The storm in his heart
demanded entry to the king's home.
True, he had been aware of feet behind him,
some going in
by a garden gate so low
it looked as if they huddled knees and spine
where crannied, star-bright flowers
mocked from a crumbling wall at the indignity.

Old as he was, he hammered on the iron door
breaking his hand,
and shouted
till the sound paled in thunder
and the high horse stamped and whinnied
and the ground threw back the shafts of frozen rain
and chilled him.

And then he fell ill
and was laid on the cold stones outside the castle
refusing to go in by
such a childish way still,
through the garden.

But lying limp on the ground
he saw himself dark-plumed and arrogant
astride his stallion
and so he shouted again at the women who took care of him :
"The door must open,
force the lock !"

The women gave him sips of honey
with their quiet hands
to ease his struggle.
And though the door refused him to the last,
sickness and pain and weakness
had driven him to such a small stature
some said they had seen him
one summer morning
running tiny and unbending as a child
under that crumbling
humbling
arch
into the garden.

SYLVIA READ

ON A DEATH IN AN OLD PEOPLE'S HOME

(To the memory of Elizabeth Williams)

I was busy, with the normal course of events,
Telephoning, actually, when they told me
"Willie's gone." A muscle in my heart
Contracted, pinched the blood,
In my throat a frog swelled.

Inevitably, with us, death
Like tea, has its routine;
The doctor, the mortician, the next of kin
Play their part in the disposal, and must be notified.

I wandered down the corridor,
Made empty by Willie's going,
A picture of the daughter in my eyes.
Pale, delicate skin, the auburn hair
Her mother's, but young and gleaming,
The soft brown eyes shattered, like pools
Whipped up by the wind, and the water spilled.

She's already taken
Some of life's punishment—
Her husband's unskilled wage,
Three small boys ambitious
For bicycles and trips with the school abroad,
And the bruising sequence of 'flu, washing, measles, shopping—
And Mum—

Her kind heart become an organ fighting
to maintain the paralytic frame,
Her capable hands deprived
Of all refined movement, her speech
Distorted and uncontrolled, with dribbling tongue;
And still behind the grotesque disabilities—
Mum—

The mind unharmed, the simple qualities
Of kindness, humour, love, all evident.

186

Willie would toddle about, a bit too fat
For her heart, and give a hand
To the more infirm; a simple joke
Would shake her frame with laughter,
A touch of trouble, in one of her letters perhaps,
Or another old lady poorly, and she would weep
With an infantile bellow and baby tears.

I could not bear
Willie to cry.
I would cradle her in my arms and beg her
Not to cry, in desperation
I would make her laugh (she laughed so easily).
I was afraid those tears, that heaving fleshy bosom,
Would release the dammed-up sorrows
Of all humanity.

I found her on her bed, the nurse
Removing pinafore, dress, stockings—
Sitting in her armchair she'd mercifully
Slipped away unknowing. I asked to help, and soon
The pale, naked body lay there, still
Limp and warm, the face calm and slowly
Smoothing out—only the hands
And fore-arms very cold. I cradled the head
For the pillow to be straightened, the grey hair patched
With flaming auburn, and wisps of nasturtium wool
Still flaring on the fair skin
Of the innocent body. Surely never

Did a body die, though limited
By low estate, tethered
To poverty all her life,
Surely never
Did one die more pure?

In the kitchen, near, a girl
Student domestic, working vacation, sobbed

Her sorrow for Willie, all her tears
Streaming along her long, long dark hair, like a flood
Of black sorrow. Suddenly,
My hand on the young bony shoulder,
Willie's hair
Burst out like a flame somewhere.

MAY IVIMY*

A DEATH ABROAD

Shake hands with time; make ready to depart
On a long journey, not at all foreseen
When first you left us, though your departing then
Foreshadowed a long absence from your friends;
And how much longer now, with no returning.
As you sink
Below the curve of our known hemisphere,
Under an alien and indifferent sky
Eternity awaits you, the long night
Shot through with unimaginable stars
That do not move to our chronologies.
From the impenetrable flesh go free;
No longer fear division of the day
Or tyranny of leaden-houred night.
The clock that ticks you hence remains to chide
Those whom you leave behind.
But while we waste this time that wasted you
Its murderous hold is broken; youth and age
No meaning have, and you can study those long silences
That are to us unknown, while the frail cord
That links us tenuously in memory
Stretches a little way, and then must snap,
Vanquished by time, that conquers us, not you.

PHYLLIS HARTNOLL

THE SCATTERING

There is snow in the air, as there is about my heart,
And my clogged feet plod through the mud in this silent place,
In the wake of the man in black with the copper urn
Which houses you in so small and dark a space.

He might be Death, as he stands in his raven gown
And for one conventional moment bows his head—
A stranger, praying a brief, impersonal prayer
For the quite unknown and so anonymous dead.

His arm swings out in a slowly widening arc,
Casting your dust as a sower scatters seed—
So small a drift to contain so much of you—
A cloud of unknowing, in my present need.

Later, the snowdrops; daffodils; the green
Of new life springing gladly where you fell.
But today the air is full of the promised snow
To shroud these ashes. I hope that all is well.

MURIEL GRAINGER

R.I.P.

Here lies a woman. Pause as you go along
    Whistling your tuneless song—
Pause and remember. What was she, man, to you?
    Faithless, false, tender, true?
Wife, mother, sweetheart? All these, perhaps and more,
    Lover or just a whore?
Whichever it was, slave, mistress, nurse or toy
    There will be no more joy.
For she is dead now—dead in more ways than one—
    She who was so much fun

And so much pain. Forget her and go your ways
    Whistling your silly phrase.

MURIEL BOX

DE MORTUIS

The quiet dead, they lie at ease
Beneath the black-plumed cypress trees,
And, in that cool and heavy bed
Fear no man's tread.
Flowers of porcelain and of beads
Vie in the grass with living weeds,
And black-plumed mourners come to pray
At close of day.
And he who stops may read and find
How good the dead men were of mind,
How chaste and yet how warm of heart
These men apart!
Husbands were faithful who lie here
And to their wives were ever dear.
Beneath a cross of stone and wood
All citizens are good.

How do we know? Read what they say,
These crosses set to mark the clay;
A race of saints, 'tis evident,
Whose course is spent. . . .

F. TENNYSON JESSE

REST

O Earth, lie heavily upon her eyes;
Seal her sweet eyes weary of watching, Earth:
Lie close around her; leave no room for mirth
With its harsh laughter, nor for sound of sighs.

She hath no questions, she hath no replies,
Hushed in and curtained with a blessed dearth
Of all that irked her from the hour of birth;
With stillness that is almost Paradise.

Darkness more clear than noonday holdeth her,
Silence more musical than any song;
Even her very heart has ceased to stir :
Until the morning of Eternity
Her rest shall not begin nor end, but be;
And when she wakes she will not think it long.

CHRISTINA ROSSETTI
(1830–1894)

Sonnet : THOU FAMISHED GRAVE

Thou famished grave, I will not fill thee yet,
Roar though thou dost, I am too happy here;
Gnaw thine own sides, fast on; I have no fear
Of thy dark project, but my heart is set
On living—I have heroes to beget
Before I die; I will not come anear
Thy dismal jaws for many a splendid year;
Till I be old I aim not to be eat.
I cannot starve thee out : I am thy prey
And thou shalt have me; but I dare defend
That I can stave thee off; and I dare say,
What with the life I lead, the force I spend,
I'll be but bones and jewels on that day,
And leave thee hungry even in the end.

EDNA ST. VINCENT MILLAY
(U.S.A.)
(1892–1950)

'SAFE IN THEIR ALABASTER CHAMBERS'

Safe in their alabaster chambers,
Untouched by morning and untouched by noon,
Sleep the meek members of the resurrection,
Rafter of satin, and roof of stone.

Light laughs the breeze in her castle of sunshine;
Babbles the bee in a stolid ear;
Pipe the sweet birds in ignorant cadence—
Ah, what sagacity perished here!

Grand go the years in the crescent above them;
Worlds scoop their arcs, and firmaments row,
Diadems drop and Doges surrender,
Soundless as dots on a disc of snow.

EMILY DICKINSON*
(U.S.A.)
(1830–1886)

THE NEW GHOST
(And he casting away his garment rose and came to Jesus.)

And he cast it down, down, on the green grass,
Over the young crocuses, where the dew was—
He cast the garment of his flesh that was full of death,
And like a sword his spirit showed out of the cold sheath.

He went a pace or two, he went to meet his Lord,
And, as I said, his spirit looked like a clean sword,
And seeing him the naked trees began shivering,
And all the birds cried out aloud as it were late spring.

And the Lord came on, He came down, and saw
That a soul was waiting there for Him, one without flaw,

And they embraced in the churchyard where the robins play,
And the daffodils hang down their heads, as they burn away.

The Lord held his head fast, and you could see
That He kissed the unsheathed ghost that was gone free—
As a hot sun, on a March day, kisses the cold ground;
And the spirit answered, for he knew well that his peace was
    found.

The spirit trembled, and sprang up at the Lord's word—
As on a wild, April day, springs a small bird—
So the ghost's feet lifting him up, he kissed the Lord's cheek,
And for the greatness of their love neither of them could speak.

But the Lord went then, to show him the way,
Over the young crocuses, under the green may
That was not quite in flower yet—to a far-distant land;
And the ghost followed, like a naked cloud holding the sun's
    hand.

FREDEGOND SHOVE*
(1889–1949)

NOTES ON POETS AND POEMS

APHRA BEHN (pp. 111–12)

The first professional woman playwright, who had the gifts and the courage to survive in an all male preserve. Her wit and gaiety pleased Charles II for whom she acted as a spy in Holland during the Dutch Wars. Her indefatigable pen turned out dozens of novels, volumes of poetry and translations as well as the plays which were very popular in her day.

ANNE BRADSTREET (p. 111)

As well as being one of the rare women writers of her period whose work survives, she has the distinction of being one of the early settlers in America. Students of the unusual might care to try the highly obscure but fascinating long poem by the contemporary American poet, John Berryman, called "Homage to Mistress Bradstreet". The reference to turtles in this poem is (as in Shakespeare's "The Phoenix and the Turtle") to the turtle dove.

THE BRONTE SISTERS (pp. 59, 61, 134)

Though Charlotte and Anne are less known as poets, it seemed worthwhile to have a poem from each. All were written when they were close to or still in their teens, and all inspired by the wild windy landscapes of their Yorkshire home. The two other poems by Emily reflect respectively the twin springs of her existence, her profound spiritual life and her love of nature.

EMILY DICKINSON (pp. 95, 141, 192)

Edward Sackville-West, in his anthology "And So To Bed" described this poet as "the woman who dropped notes to her dearest friends out of the window on the end of a string; who spoke, by preference, through a door ajar; who nursed a wound so secret that—like a phrase of music—it keeps its mystery to this day."

MONICA DITMAS (*Annunciation*) (p. 175)

This poem was one of the prize-winning entries in the Cheltenham Festival in 1966.

ROSEMARY DOBSON (*Country Press*) (p. 49)

The line "Oh, *Western Star* that bringest all to fold" comes from one of Sappho's poems.

'MICHAEL FIELD' (pp. 99, 109–10)

This pseudonym conceals the identity of two ladies, Miss Katherine Bradley and Miss Edith Cooper, who were aunt and niece. They lived devotedly together, producing some fourteen volumes of poems and verse plays which earned the praise of their contemporaries, and died of cancer within a few months of each other. In the poem "And on my eyes dark sleep by night" the name Phaon is a reference to the boatman Sappho is said to have loved, and the title is a fragment of her verse.

JILL FURSE (p. 98)

Best known as a beautiful actress, she died young of an obscure disease. She was married to Laurence Whistler, poet and glass engraver who has written the story of their love in "The Initials in the Heart" and recently published her poems under the title "To Celebrate her Living".

KATHLEEN HERBERT (*The Virgin Capture*) (p. 72)

This poem was one of the winning entries in the Stroud Festival in 1967. It refers to the medieval legend that a unicorn could only be caught by a virgin, in whose lap he would mildly lay his head.

MAY IVIMY (*On a Death in an Old People's Home*) (p. 186)

This poem appeared in the collection "Midway This Path" which won the Manifold Chapbook Competition in 1966.

MARGUERITE JOHANSEN (*High-Heeled Boots*) (p. 23)

This poem won the Ibberson Jones Trophy (Swindon) in 1965.

ANGELLA LANGFIELD (*The Chariot—Giacometti*) (p. 167)

Those who have seen Giacometti's sculptures will appreciate the aptness of this evocation. One line "fleshless levels fat Olympus" may seem baffling but is explained by the writer thus: this pared-down goddess makes the fleshly— literally and metaphorically—Olympians seem mundane, insignificant.

197

AMY LOWELL (p. 151)

A member of the distinguished Boston literary family referred to in the couplet :

"The Cabots talk only to the Lowells
And the Lowells talk only to God"

Living in the town where the Boston Tea Party took place, no doubt she was familiar with the tall clippers from the East coming to anchor in the harbour.

CHARLOTTE MEW (p. 118)

One of the saddest figures in literary history, Charlotte Mew fought a losing struggle with poverty, nursed and lost a loved invalid sister and did what she could for "fallen women". She was a small indomitable woman, something of an eccentric, appearing in clothes of mannish cut with a stern umbrella at Harold Munro's Poetry Bookshop where poets forgathered. She was eventually granted a small Civil List pension but ended her own life at the age of 59. Her output is small but extraordinary.

EDNA ST. VINCENT MILLAY (pp. 37, 191)

One of the greatest and most prolific of American poets— a beautiful, brilliant and spirited figure in her lifetime— her sonnets alone would suffice to have earned her a lasting reputation, particularly the long sequences, "Fatal Interview", "Sonnets from an Ungrafted Tree" and "Epitaph for the Race of Man".

MARIANNE MOORE (p. 145)

A major figure in the world of poetry, who has carried off all the big awards in the U.S.A. and been showered with honours. Her highly individual and forthright style makes it hard to realize she was born as long ago as 1887.

CAROLINE NORTON (p. 113)

A granddaughter of the actor Sheridan and inspiration for Meredith's novel "Diana of the Crossways". Her unfortunate marriage to George Norton and subsequent litigation, in which she fought with spirit and against much hostility, led in the end to the Marriage Reform Bill, granting women their first step towards legal status. She published a number of novels, six books of poems and several children's books, and edited and largely wrote various popular periodicals of her day.

MOIRA O'NEILL (p. 115)
This was the pen-name of Agnes Shakespeare Higginson born of Irish parentage in the island of Mauritius.

SYLVIA PLATH (pp. 33, 131)
This American writer was married to another poet, Ted Hughes. After a period of mental illness she took her own life in her early thirties, but not before she had established a reputation as a poet of striking ability.

VICTORIA SACKVILLE-WEST (pp. 45, 94)
Wife of the diplomat Harold Nicolson, she lived in Sissinghurst Castle which they restored from the ruins of Civil War days and surrounded with exquisite gardens open to the public. She wrote a number of novels and poems including the two long book-length ones "The Land" and "The Garden".

SAPPHO (p. 157)
The first woman poet, whose work survives only in fragments except for this ode. In the sixth century B.C. on the island of Lesbos she ran a finishing school where young women were taught to dance and sing and play the lute. It has been pointed out that she would hardly have been entrusted with the care of their daughters by the best Hellenic families of the time if she had been given to the practices named after her island.

The translator of this ode was instrumental in raising funds for commissioning the statue of Sappho recently unveiled in the poet's birthplace, Mitylene on Lesbos, and now lives there permanently.

(See also two fragments from Sappho's verse in the poems on pages 49 and 109.)

FREDEGOND SHOVE (*The New Ghost*) (p. 192)
There is a fine setting of this poem by Ralph Vaughan Williams, who was her uncle by marriage.

JAN STRUTHER (p. 104)

Actually J. Anstruther, she wrote a delightful column in "The Times" for many years under the title "Mrs. Miniver's Diary", subsequently published a book "Mrs. Miniver" in the same form, and wrote the script for the film about Mrs. Miniver's experiences in the war.

HELEN WADDELL (pp. 77, 108)

The decision not to include translations (except in the case of Sappho) has been broken in this instance as Helen Waddell's "Medieval Latin Lyrics" have become part of our literary heritage. Though the original MSS found in the abbeys were written by monks, her translations may well be said to have achieved existence in their own right and thus to be eligible for inclusion here. The companion volume to the "Medieval Latin Lyrics", "The Wandering Scholars" and her novel "Peter Abelard" are remarkable works.

AUTHOR'S INDEX

203

INDEX TO FIRST LINES

206